Schools, Churches, Social Clubs, Civic Clubs, Boys and Girls Groups, Youth Groups, Class Groups
Please call for appointment 580-478-3534. Visits to the Gallery are FREE - 7th and Walnut – Fairview, OK

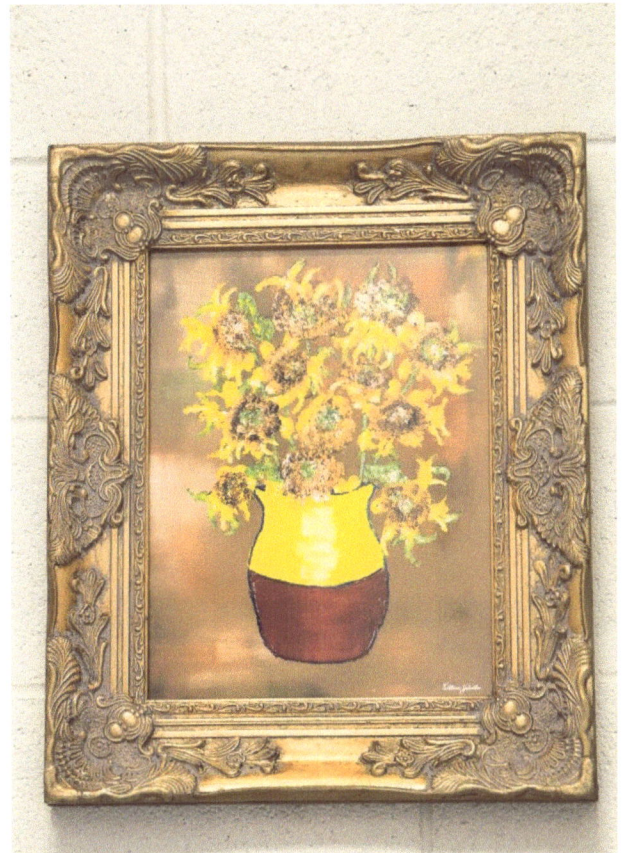
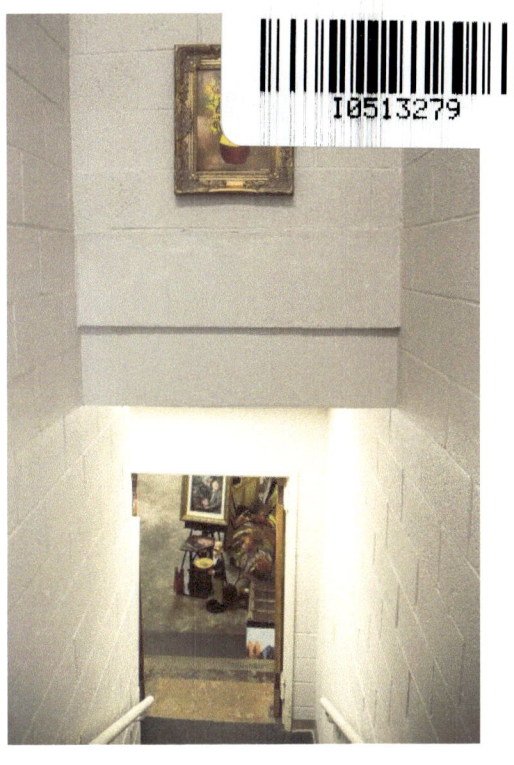
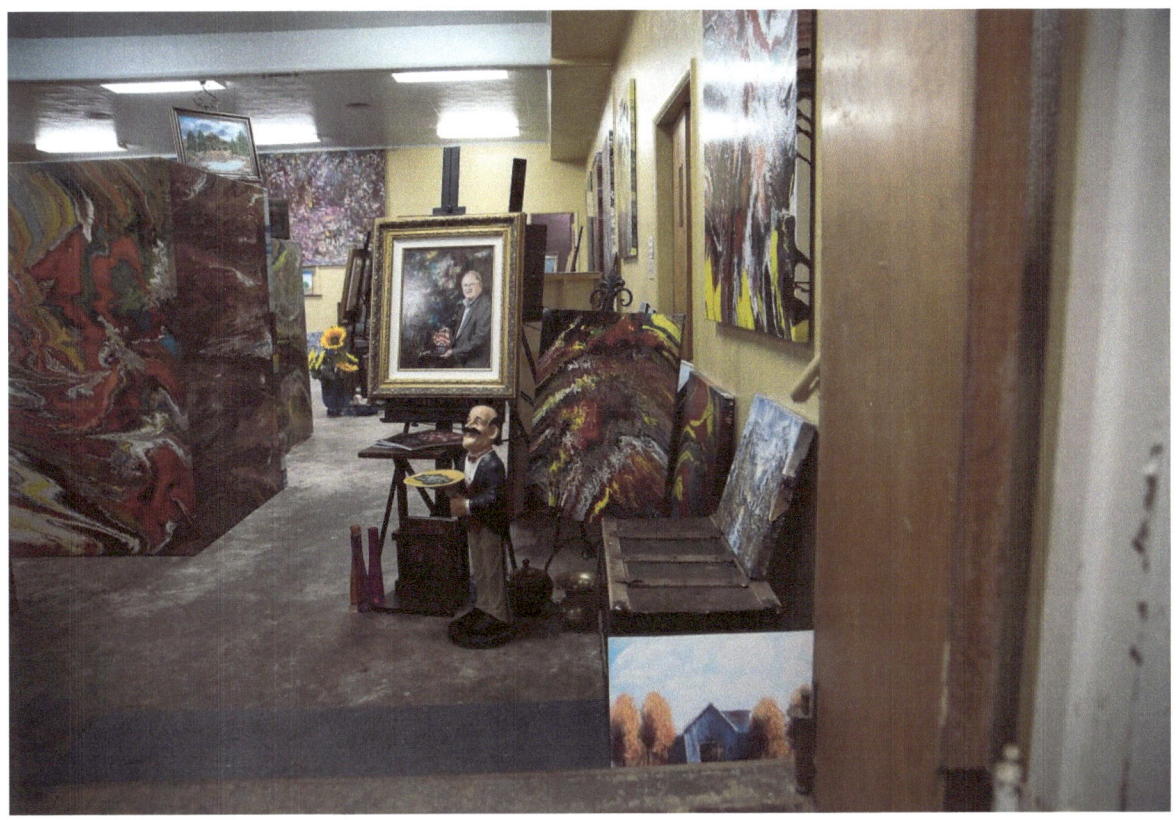

Schools, Churches, Social Clubs, Civic Clubs, Boys and Girls Groups, Youth Groups, Class Groups
Please call for appointment 580-478-3534. Visits to the Gallery are FREE - 7th and Walnut – Fairview, OK

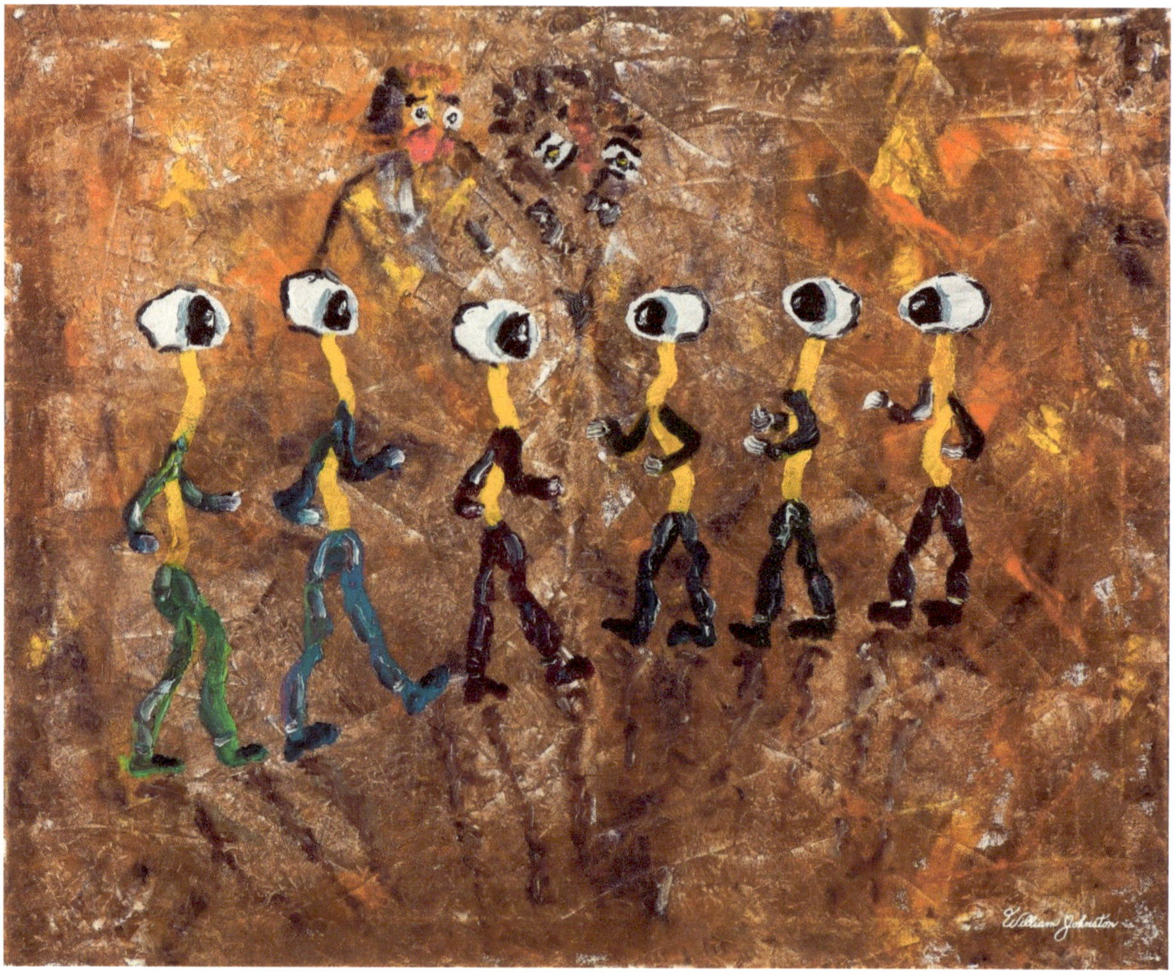

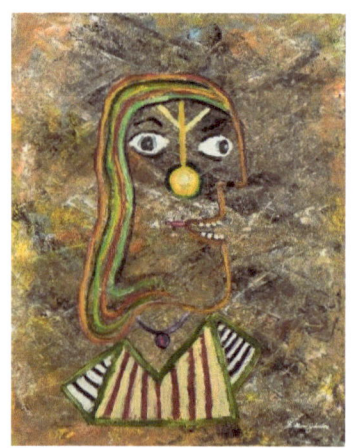
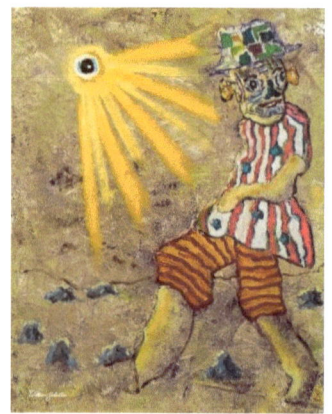
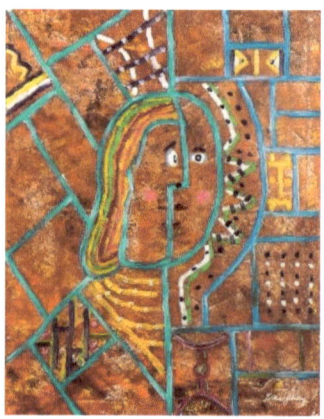

Schools, Churches, Social Clubs, Civic Clubs, Boys and Girls Groups, Youth Groups, Class Groups
Please call for appointment 580-478-3534. Visits to the Gallery are FREE - 7th and Walnut – Fairview, OK

This is your invitation to visit the Vincent Van Gogh "Leap of Faith" Gallery in Fairview, Oklahoma

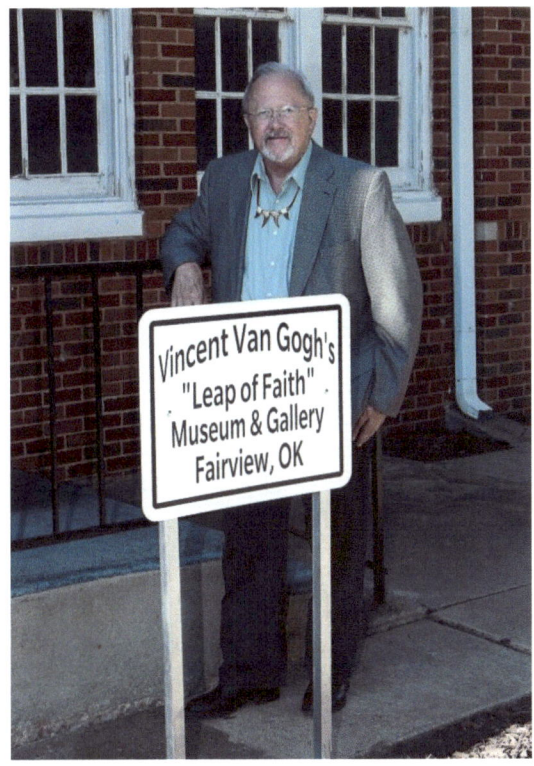

William Johnston

William Johnston is an abstract expressionist known for his distinct, fractal-esque style that works to "fill the mind with inspiration." His paintings are multifaceted and resemble both landscapes and portraits, although they firmly remain in the realm of the abstract. Johnston states that "thousands of images are found in his work," hinting at the resolution and depth that characterize his paintings. This depth is emphasized through the intense marbling Johnston applies to his oil paints, which allows him to retain the lively, saturated quality of his work.

In his attempt to capture an almost Biblical grandiosity, Johnston has turned his work towards both the organic and the synthetic. His intricate patterns hearken to the natural complexity of organic forms while also insistently hinting at the future possibilities of the digital world.

Johnston shows the influence of the vast landscapes of the American Southwest. He has become 'America's Artist. His artwork introduces a new form of oil painting that includes the technique of Jackson Pollock, the charm of Vincent Van Gogh, the reflective imagination of Claud Monet and the free style of Gerhard Richter. It is said he paints with a divine heart and calls the viewers to search down deep for meaning. History will record that he has captured a spiritual reflection in his paintings and that he has taken a 'Leap of Faith.' These are truly remarkable paintings the likes of which have never been seen or felt before. Exhibits include Banks and Educational Institutions, The Seven State Biennial Exhibition, The Nesbitt Gallery, The Charles B. Goddard Center, The Red River Museum and Agora Gallery in New York City.

William Johnston drew as a young man and painted landscapes with watercolors but did not oil paint until his early sixties when he completed many of his best known works: The Card Players, Heaven's Gate, The Grand View, Water lily Pond, The Last Supper, and The Sower to name a few.

Schools, Churches, Social Clubs, Civic Clubs, Boys and Girls Groups, Youth Groups, Class Groups Please call for appointment 580-478-3534. Visits to the Gallery are FREE - 7th and Walnut – Fairview, OK

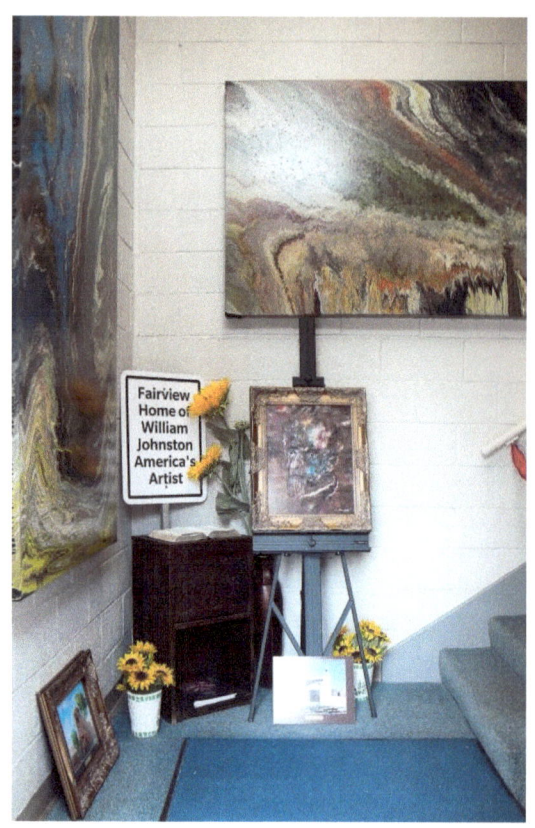

Fire of Faith

The Fire of Faith is kindled this day

By the flowers so softly given,

To teach the heart to be a part

Of a spirit never broken.

The Fire of Faith guides this hand

So lovingly touched with colors bright,

So when in need reach out and touch the Fire of Faith

Given as He has spoken.

by William Johnston

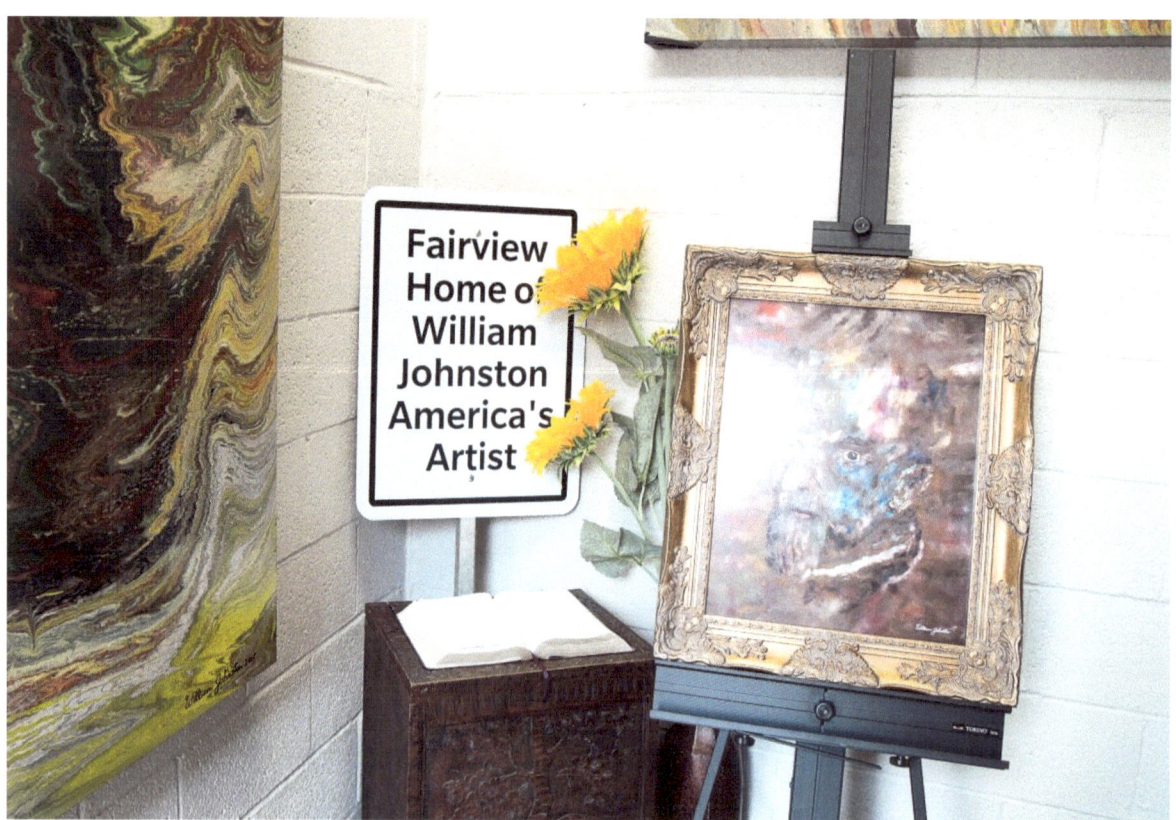

Schools, Churches, Social Clubs, Civic Clubs, Boys and Girls Groups, Youth Groups, Class Groups
Please call for appointment 580-478-3534. Visits to the Gallery are FREE - 7th and Walnut – Fairview, OK

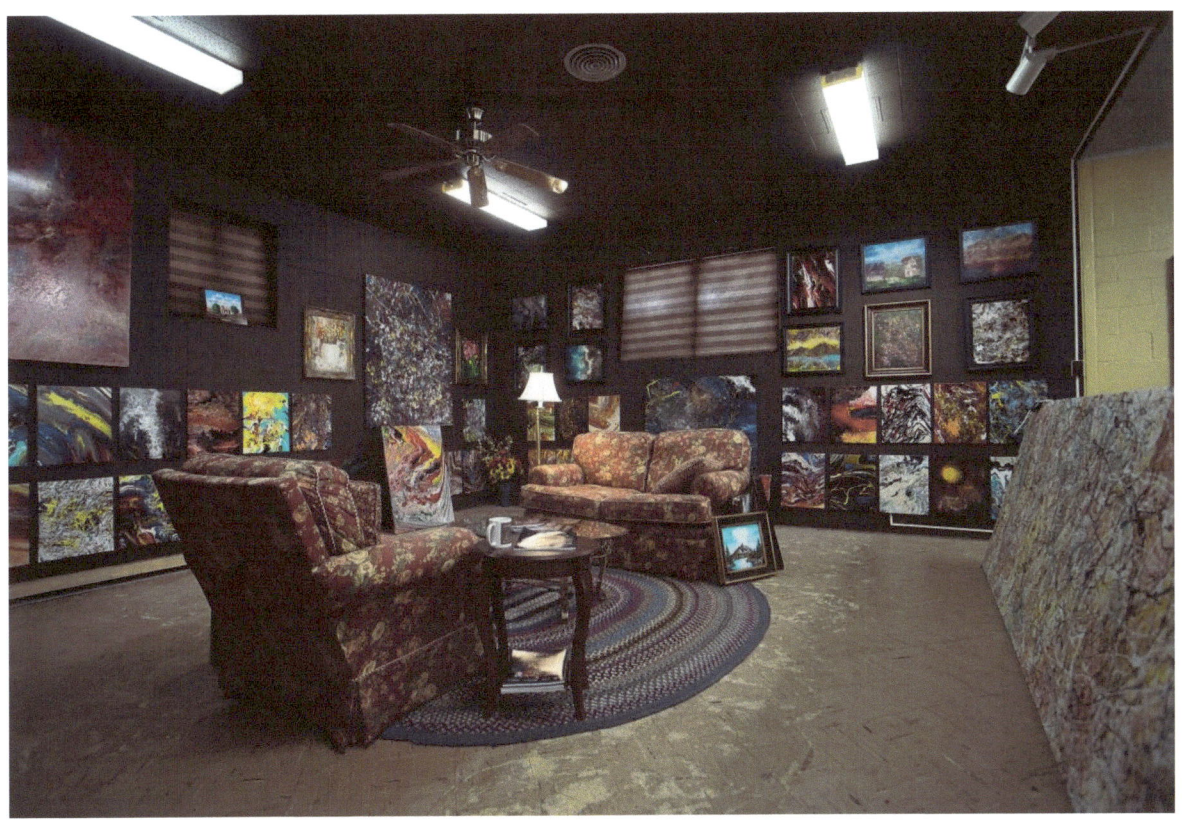

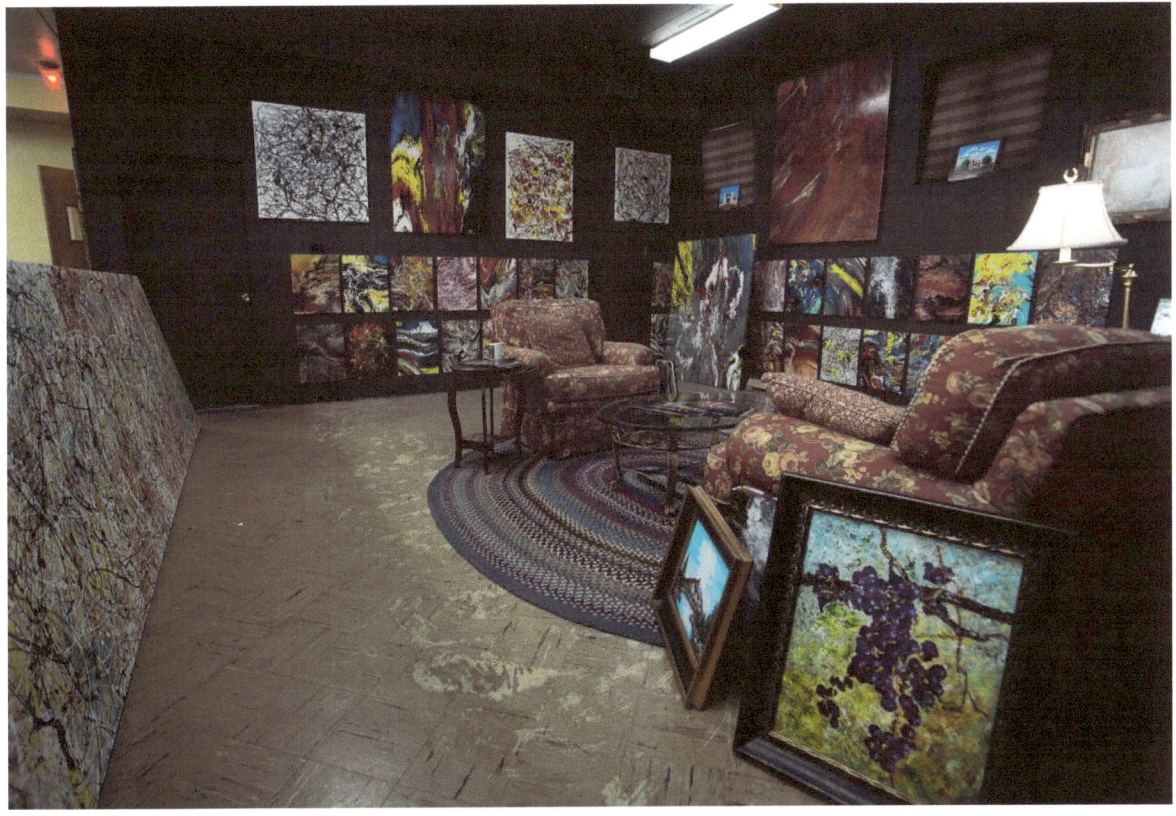

Schools, Churches, Social Clubs, Civic Clubs, Boys and Girls Groups, Youth Groups, Class Groups
Please call for appointment 580-478-3534. Visits to the Gallery are FREE - 7th and Walnut – Fairview, OK

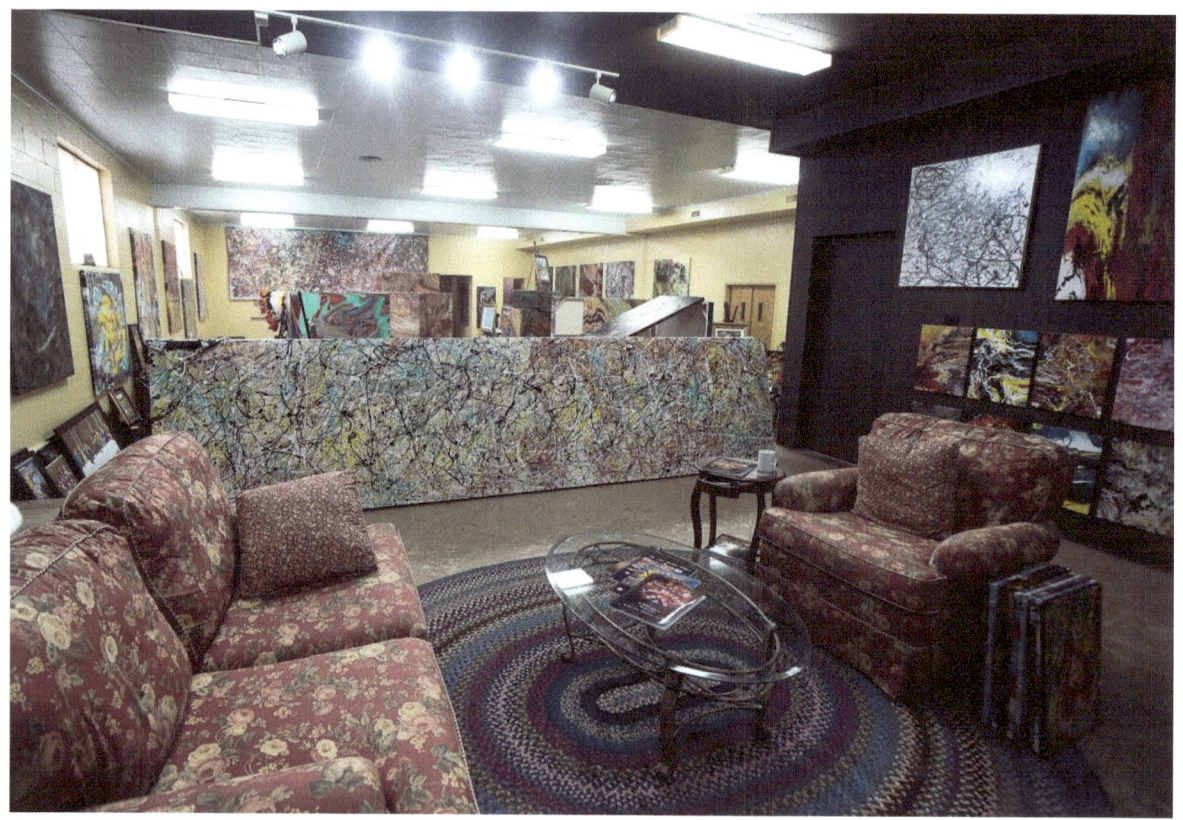

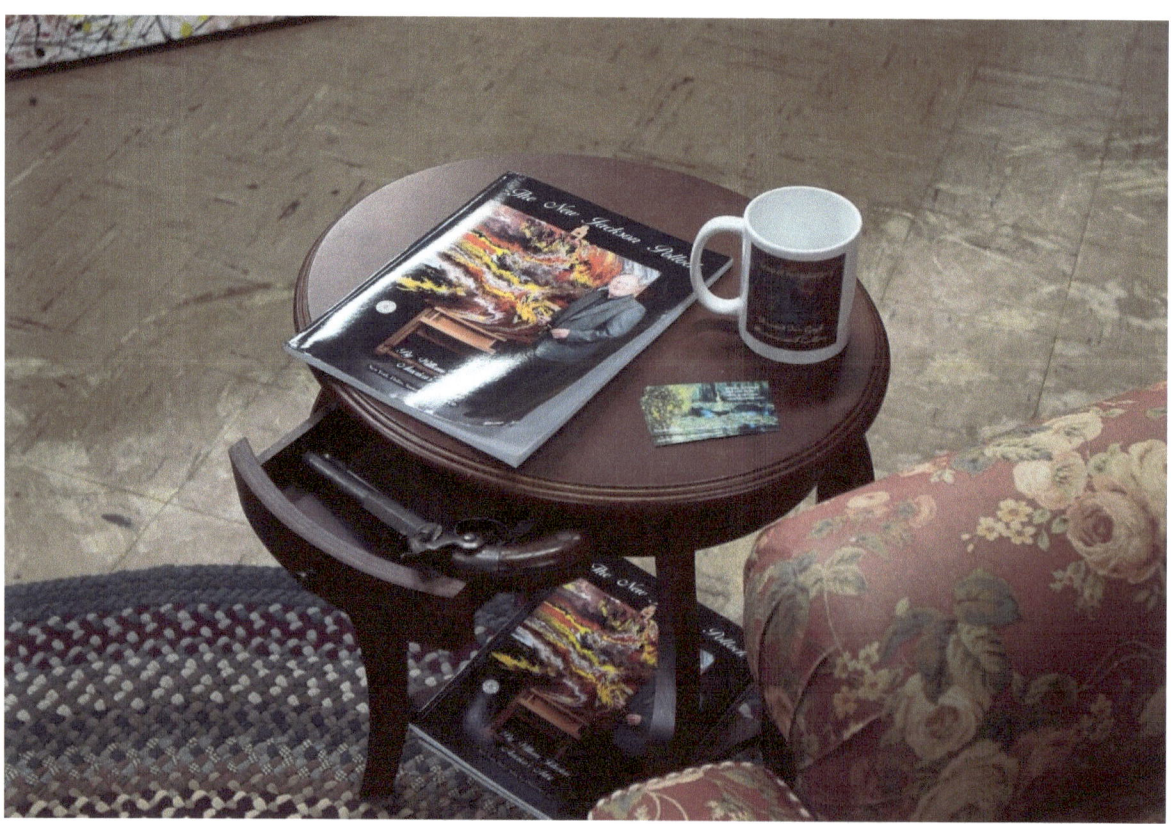

Schools, Churches, Social Clubs, Civic Clubs, Boys and Girls Groups, Youth Groups, Class Groups
Please call for appointment 580-478-3534. Visits to the Gallery are FREE - 7th and Walnut – Fairview, OK

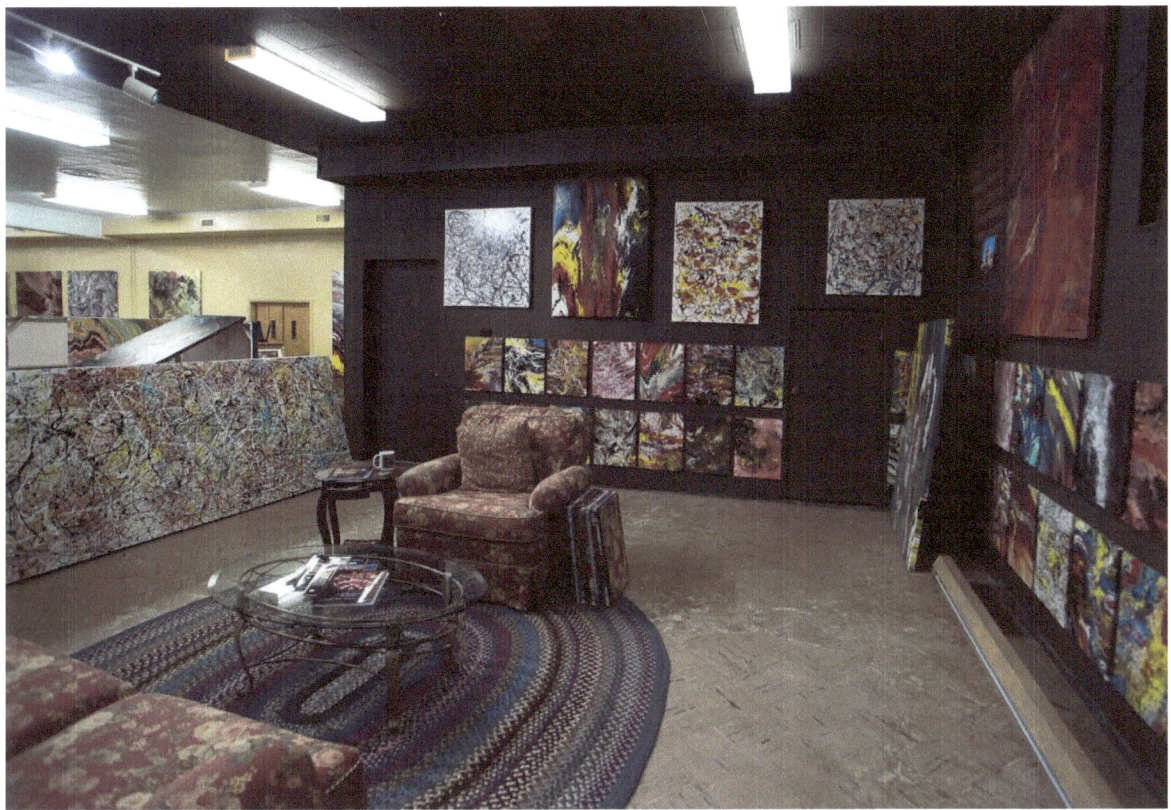

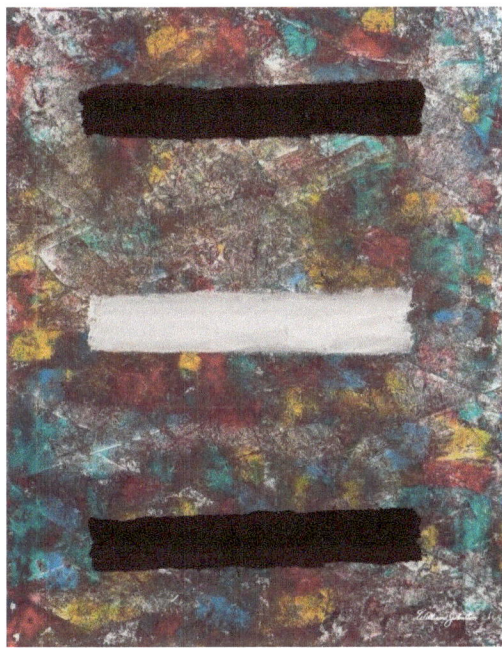

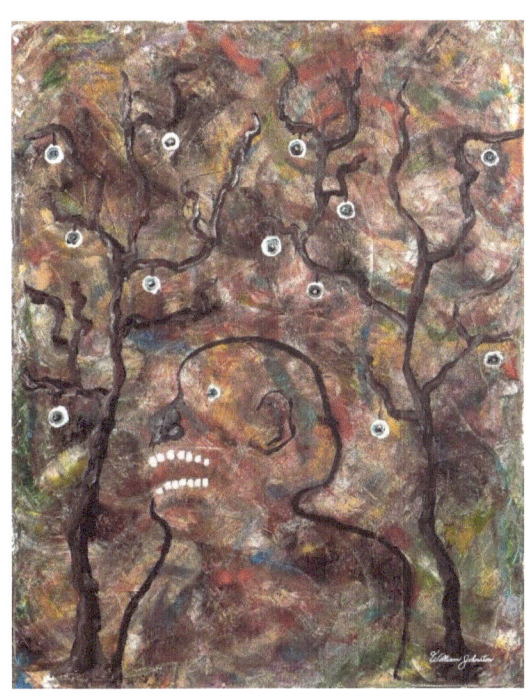

Schools, Churches, Social Clubs, Civic Clubs, Boys and Girls Groups, Youth Groups, Class Groups
Please call for appointment 580-478-3534. Visits to the Gallery are FREE - 7th and Walnut – Fairview, OK

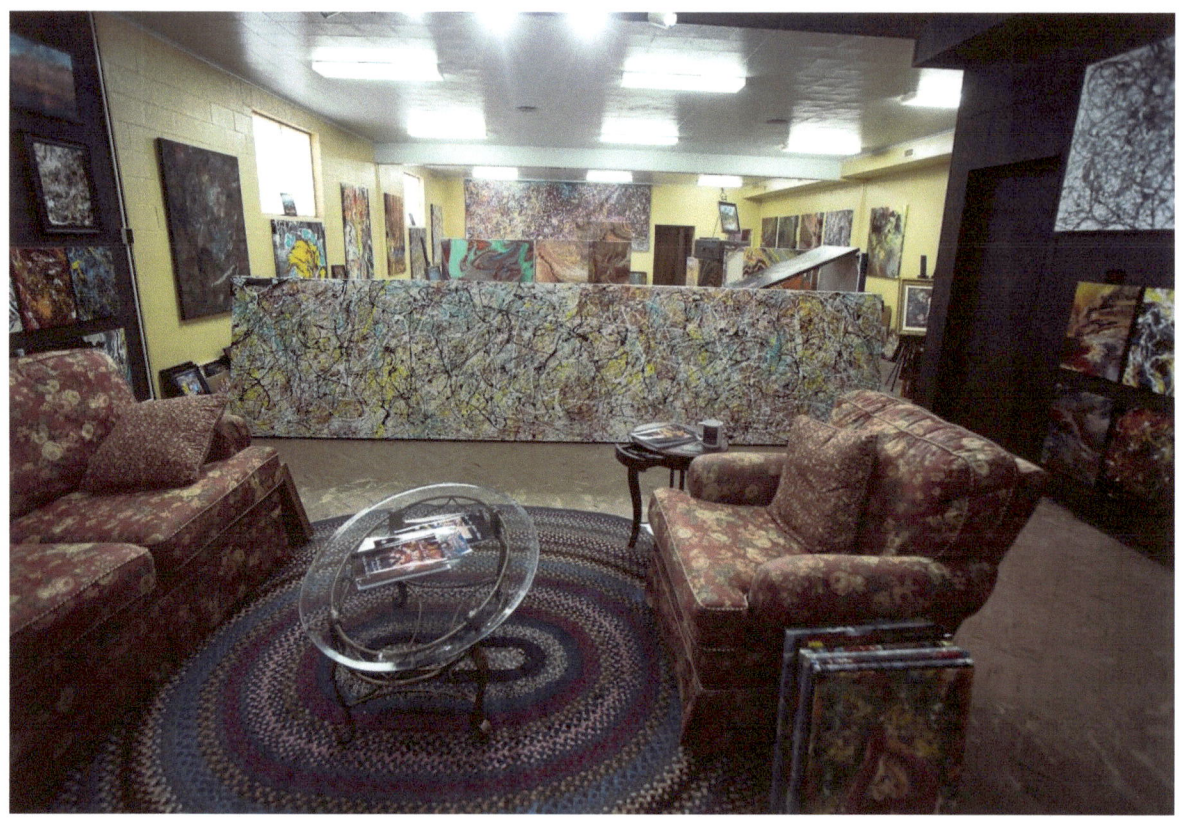

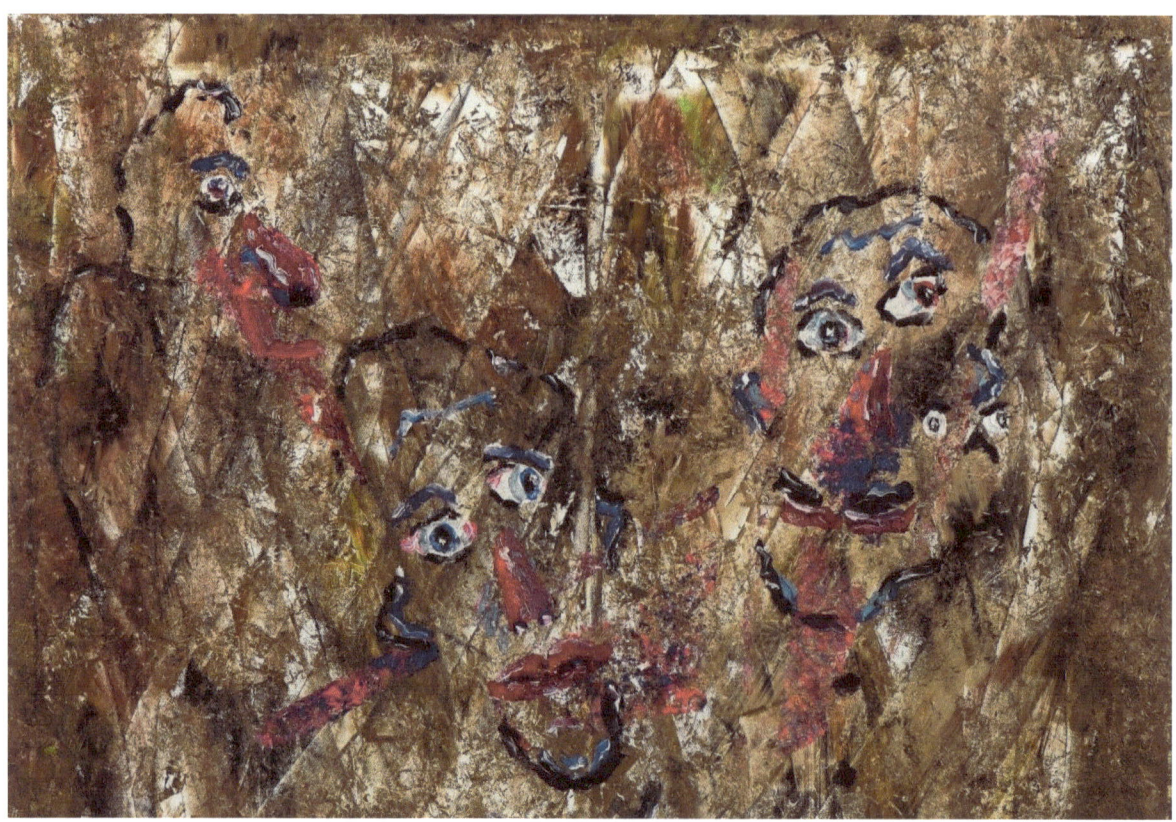

Schools, Churches, Social Clubs, Civic Clubs, Boys and Girls Groups, Youth Groups, Class Groups
Please call for appointment 580-478-3534. Visits to the Gallery are FREE - 7th and Walnut – Fairview, OK

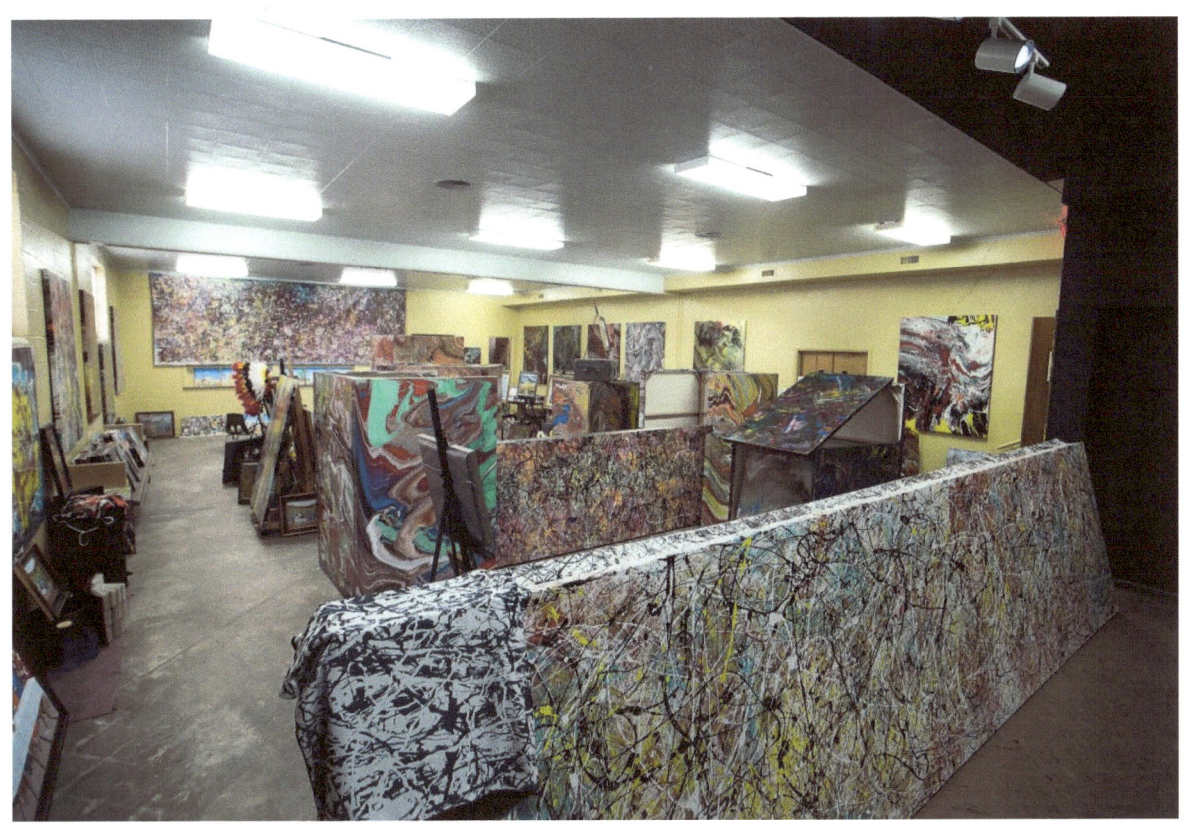

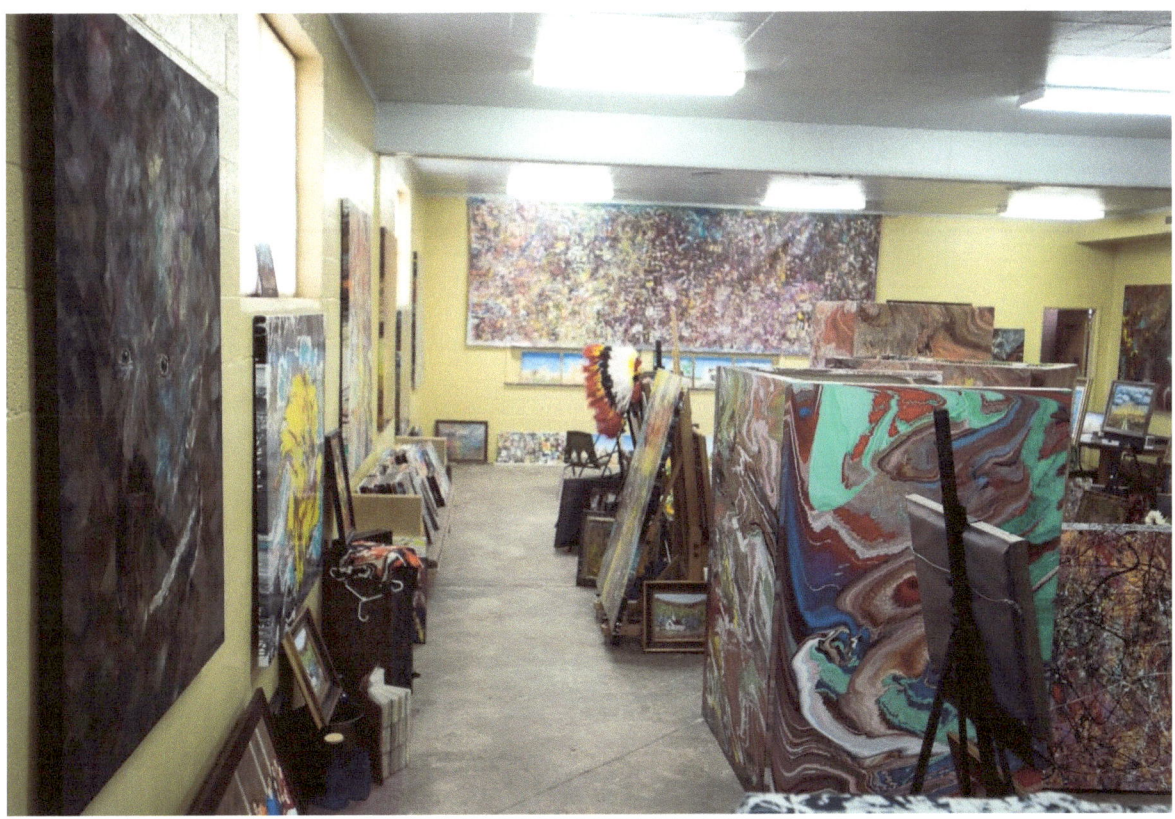

Schools, Churches, Social Clubs, Civic Clubs, Boys and Girls Groups, Youth Groups, Class Groups
Please call for appointment 580-478-3534. Visits to the Gallery are FREE - 7th and Walnut – Fairview, OK

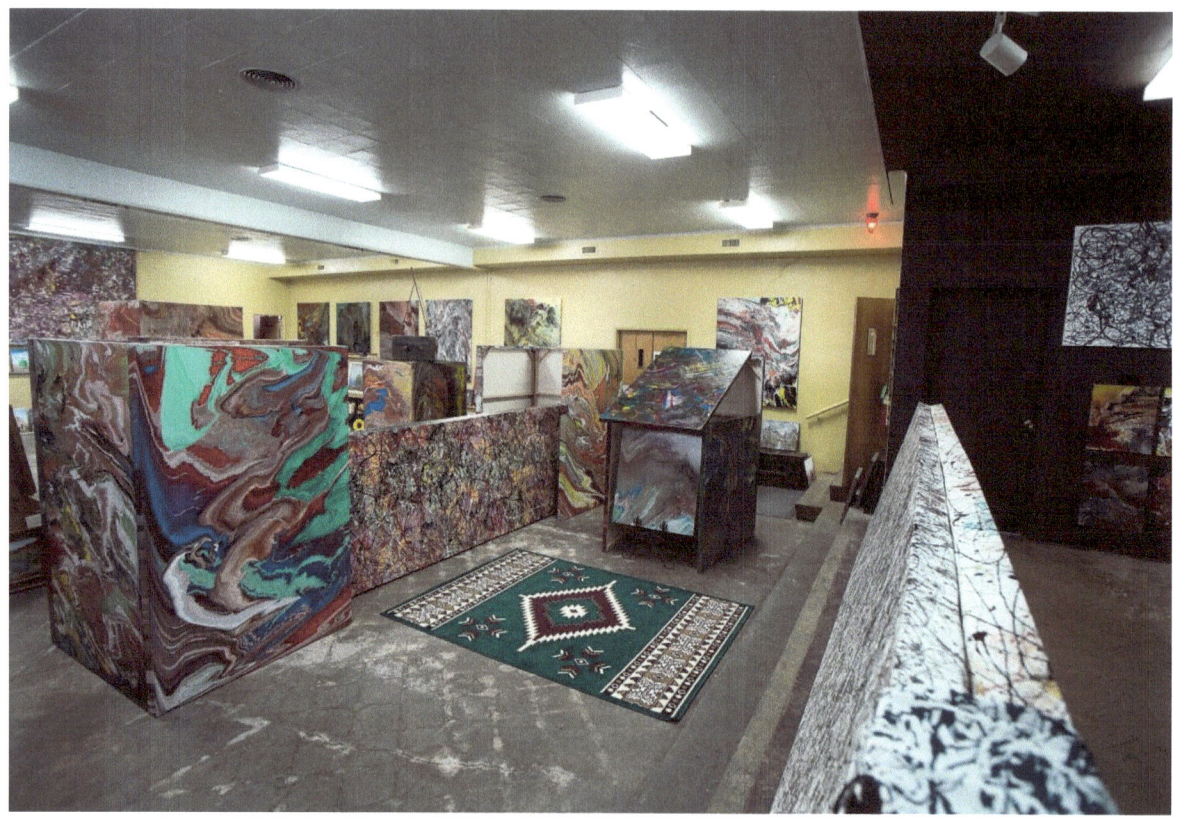

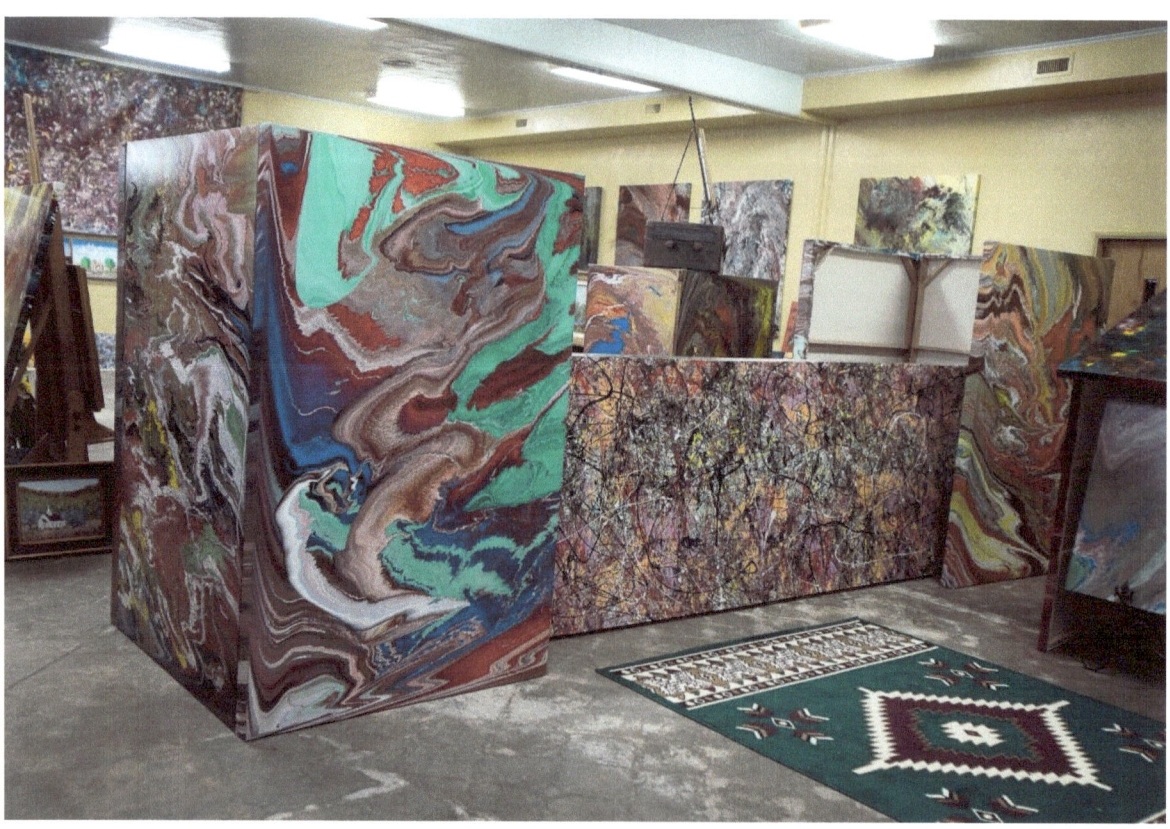

Schools, Churches, Social Clubs, Civic Clubs, Boys and Girls Groups, Youth Groups, Class Groups
Please call for appointment 580-478-3534. Visits to the Gallery are FREE - 7th and Walnut – Fairview, OK

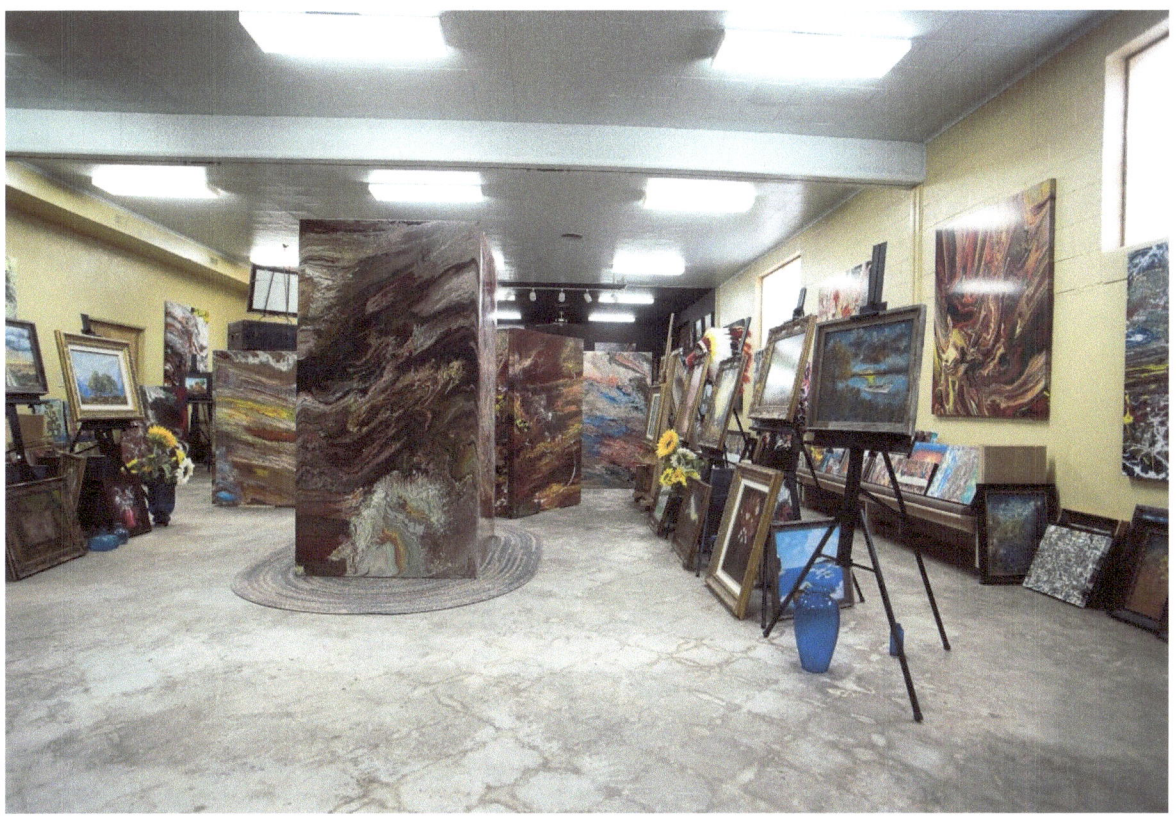

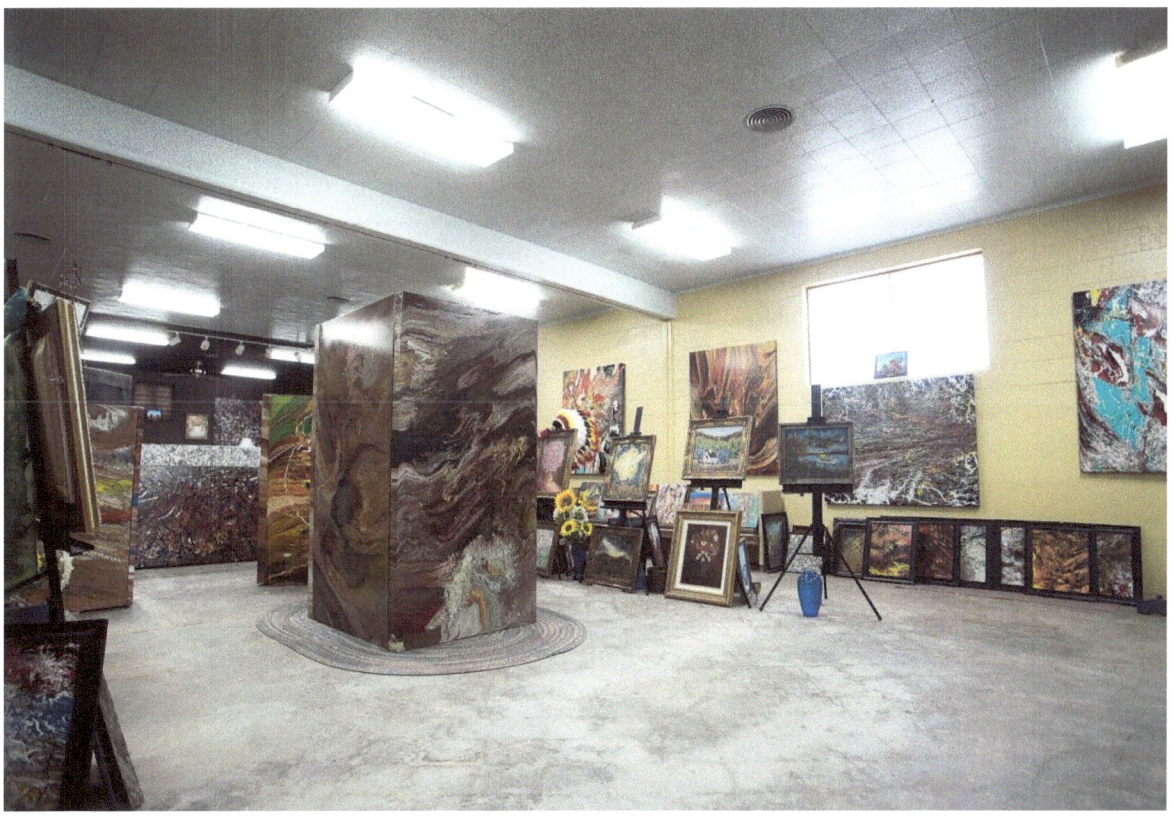

Schools, Churches, Social Clubs, Civic Clubs, Boys and Girls Groups, Youth Groups, Class Groups
Please call for appointment 580-478-3534. Visits to the Gallery are FREE - 7th and Walnut – Fairview, OK

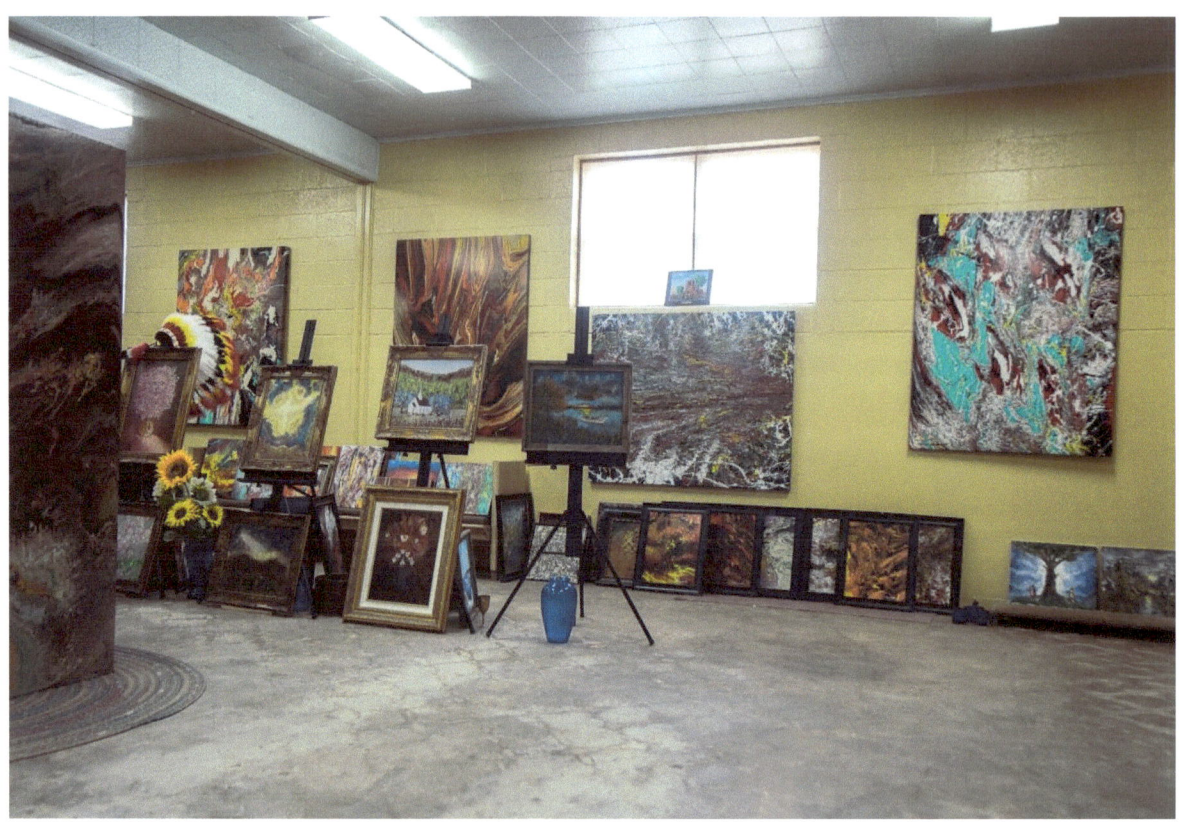

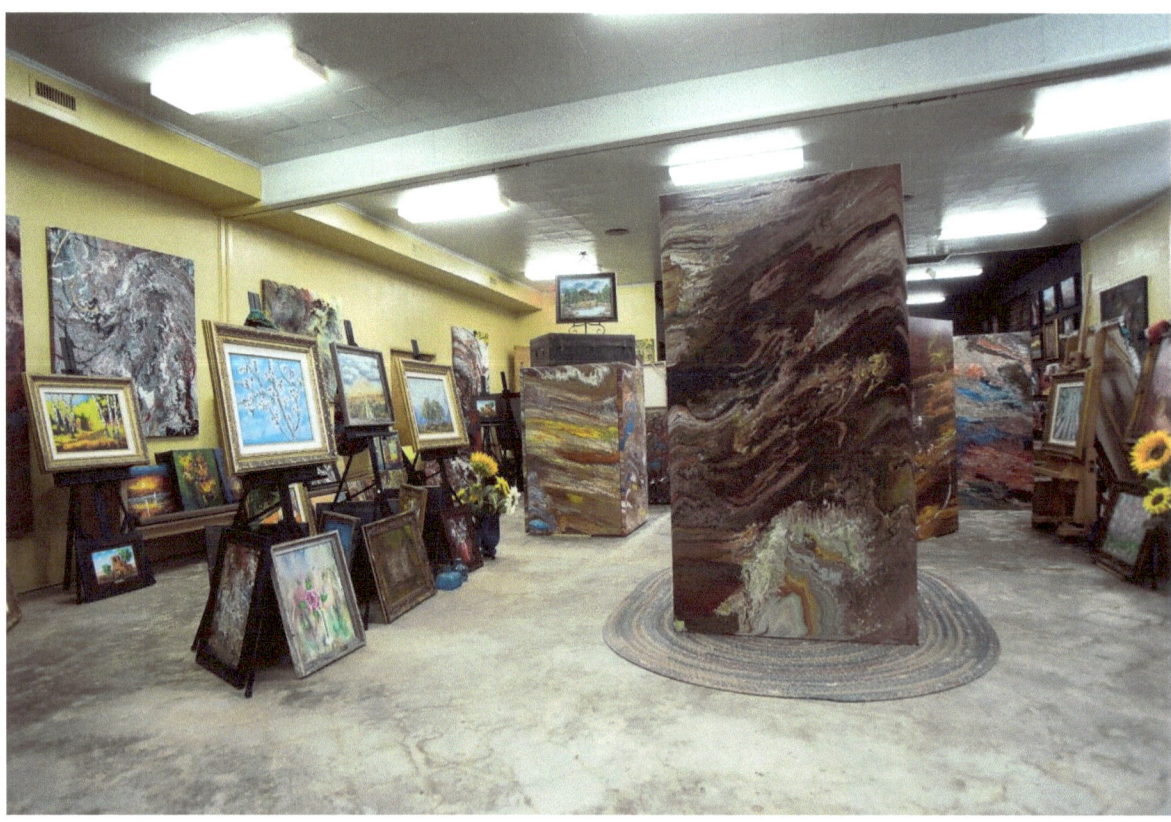

Schools, Churches, Social Clubs, Civic Clubs, Boys and Girls Groups, Youth Groups, Class Groups
Please call for appointment 580-478-3534. Visits to the Gallery are FREE - 7th and Walnut – Fairview, OK

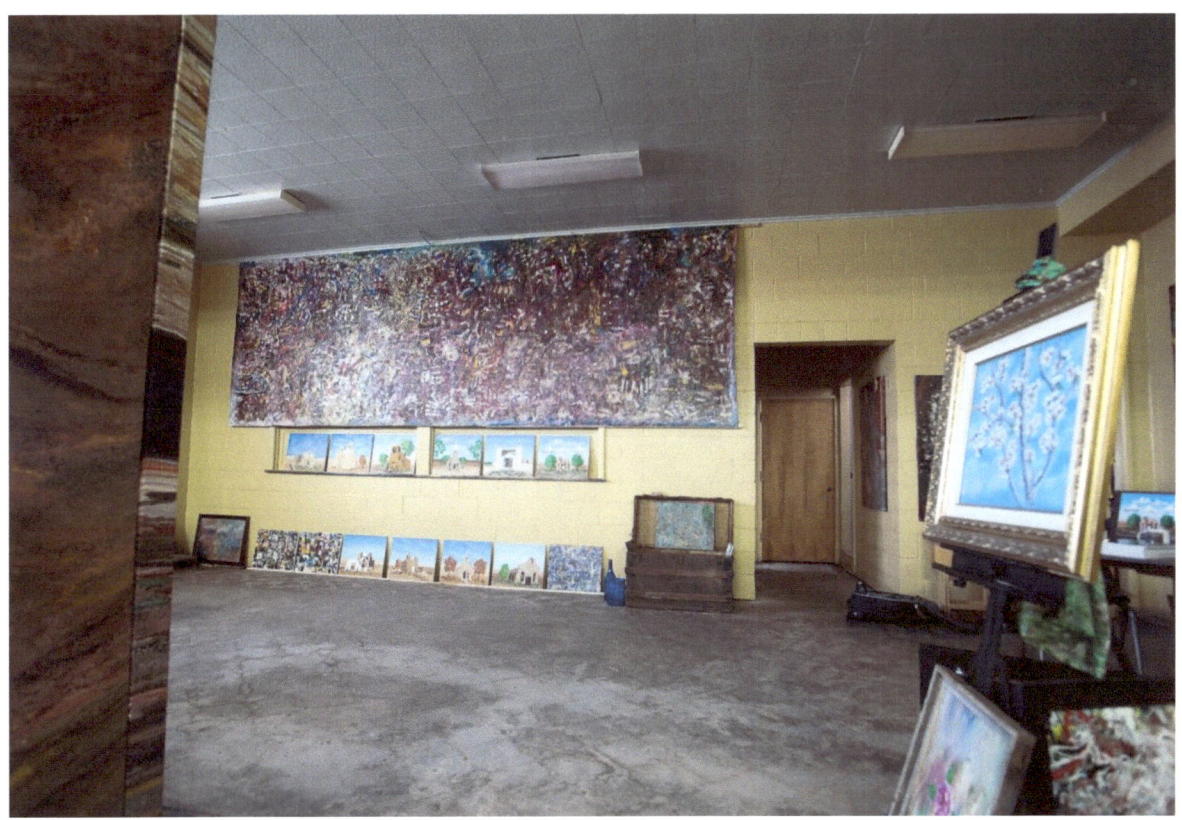

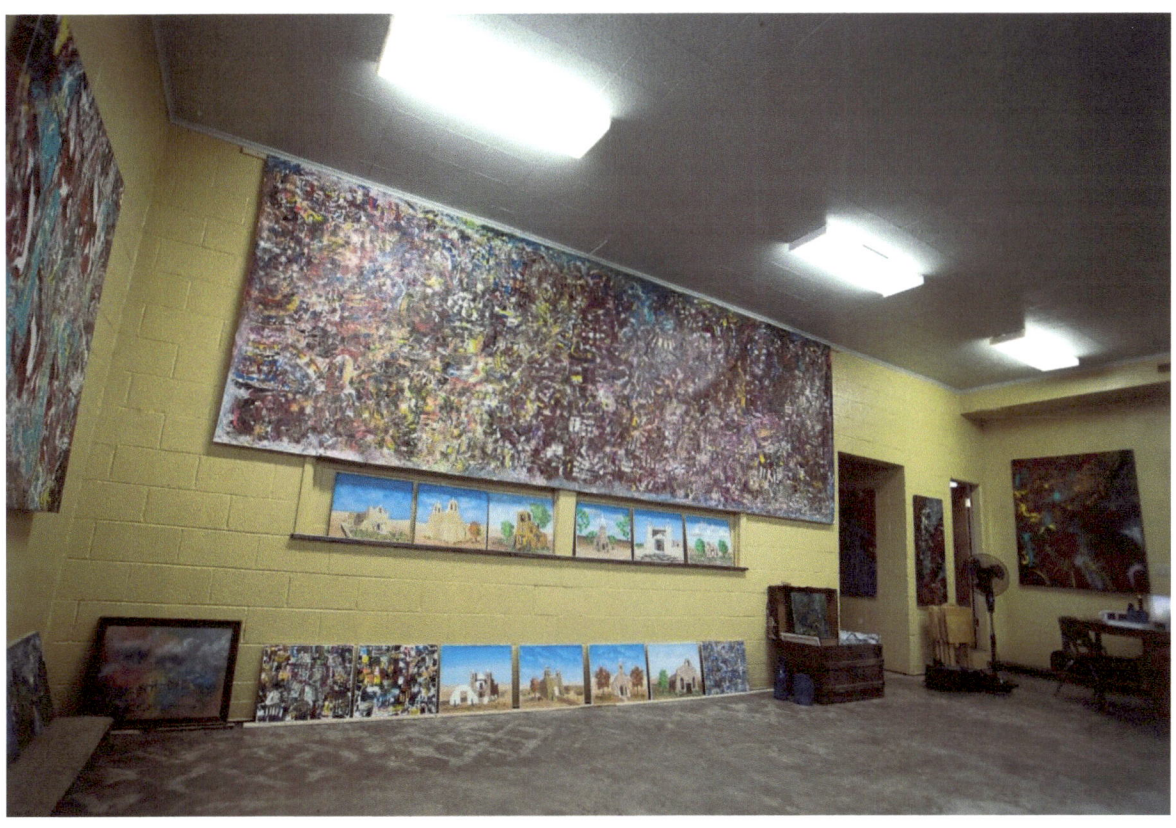

Schools, Churches, Social Clubs, Civic Clubs, Boys and Girls Groups, Youth Groups, Class Groups
Please call for appointment 580-478-3534. Visits to the Gallery are FREE - 7th and Walnut – Fairview, OK

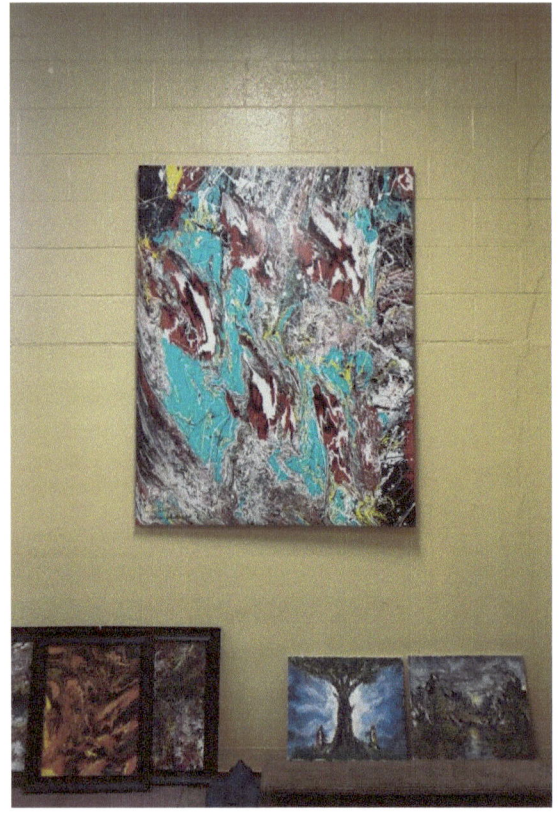

Tossed with rough winds and faint with fear,
Above the tempest soft and clear
What still small accents greet mine ear
't Is I, be not afraid.'

't Is I, who washed thy spirit white;
't Is I, who gave thy blind eyes sight,
't Is I, thy Lord, thy life, thy light,
't Is I, be not afraid. '

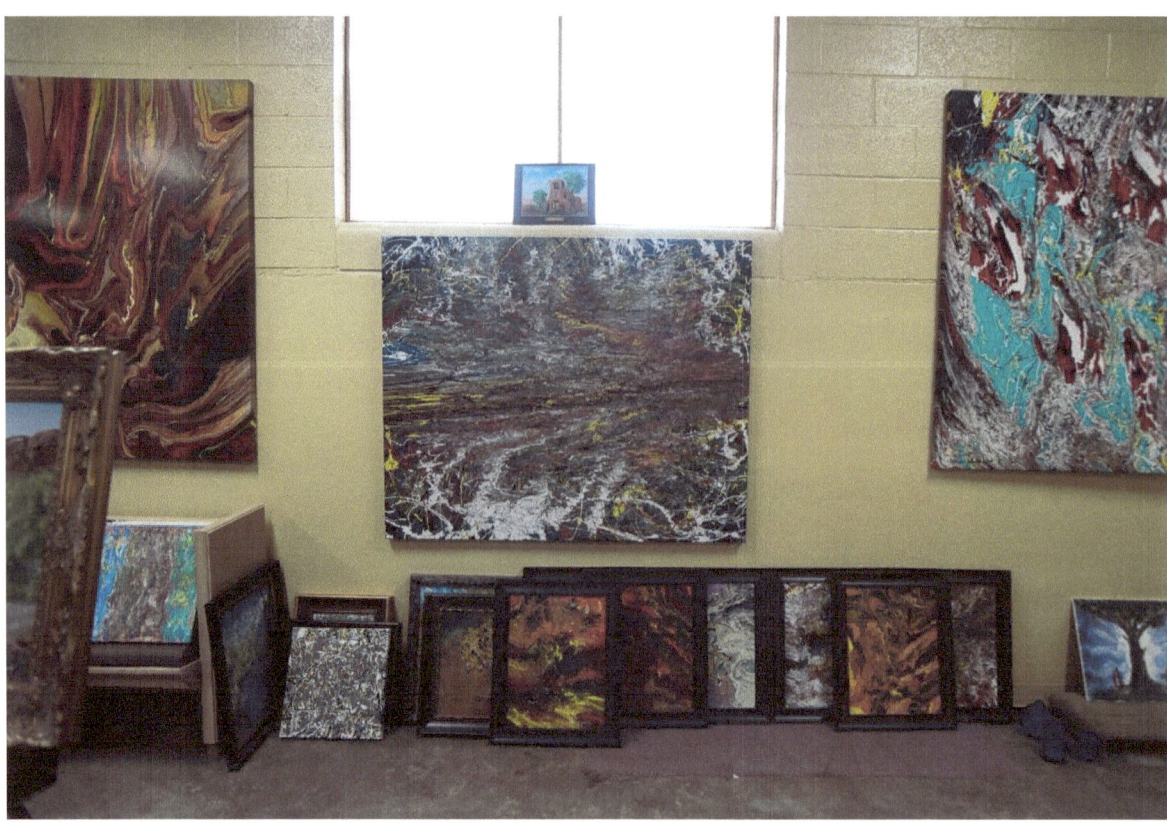

Schools, Churches, Social Clubs, Civic Clubs, Boys and Girls Groups, Youth Groups, Class Groups
Please call for appointment 580-478-3534. Visits to the Gallery are FREE - 7th and Walnut – Fairview, OK

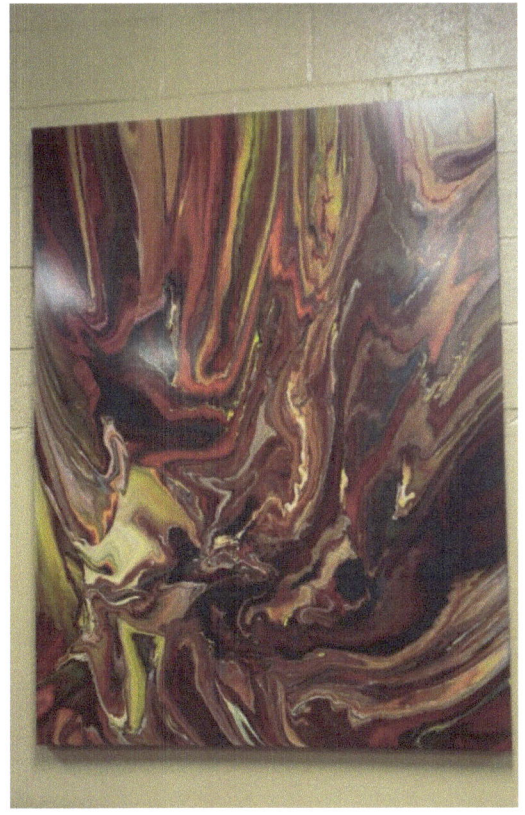

This bitter cup, I drank it first
To thee it is no draught accurst
The hand that gives it thee is pierced
't Is I, be not afraid. '

When on the other side thy feet,
Shall rest, mid thousand welcomes sweet;
One well known voice thy heart shall greet –
't Is I, be not afraid. '

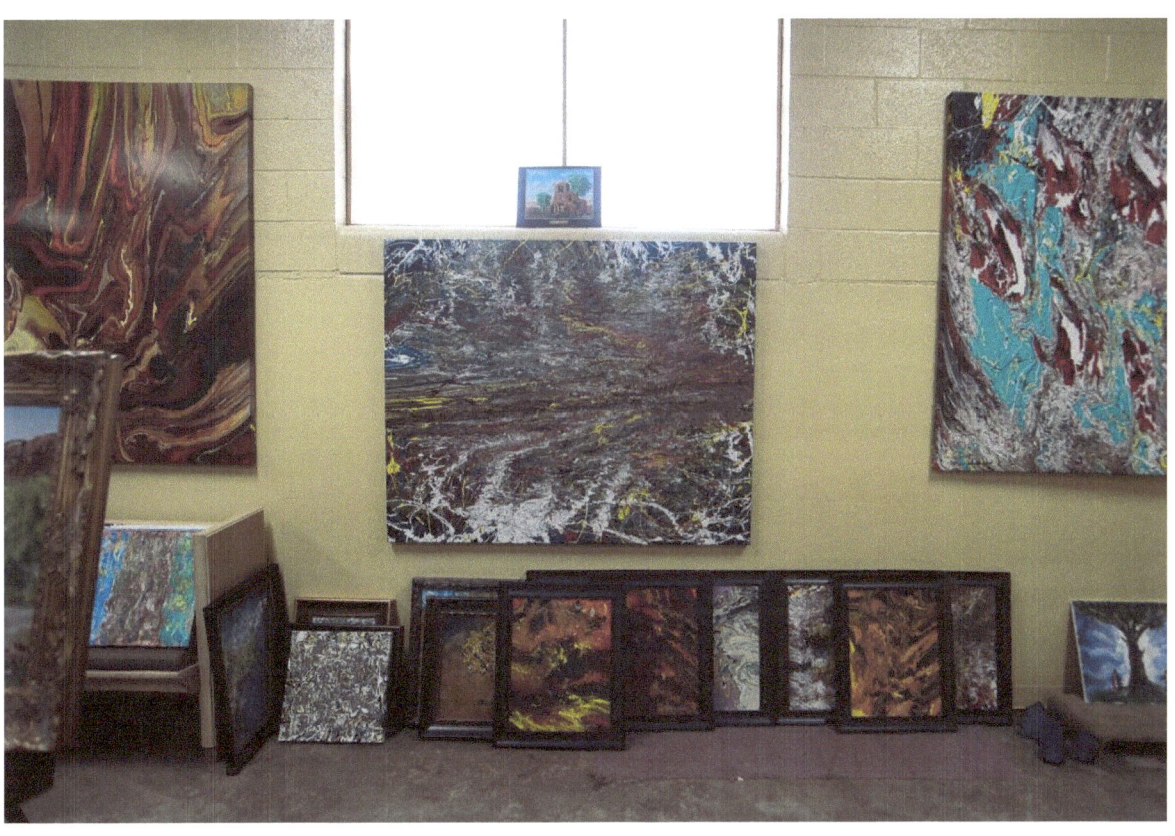

Schools, Churches, Social Clubs, Civic Clubs, Boys and Girls Groups, Youth Groups, Class Groups
Please call for appointment 580-478-3534. Visits to the Gallery are FREE - 7th and Walnut – Fairview, OK

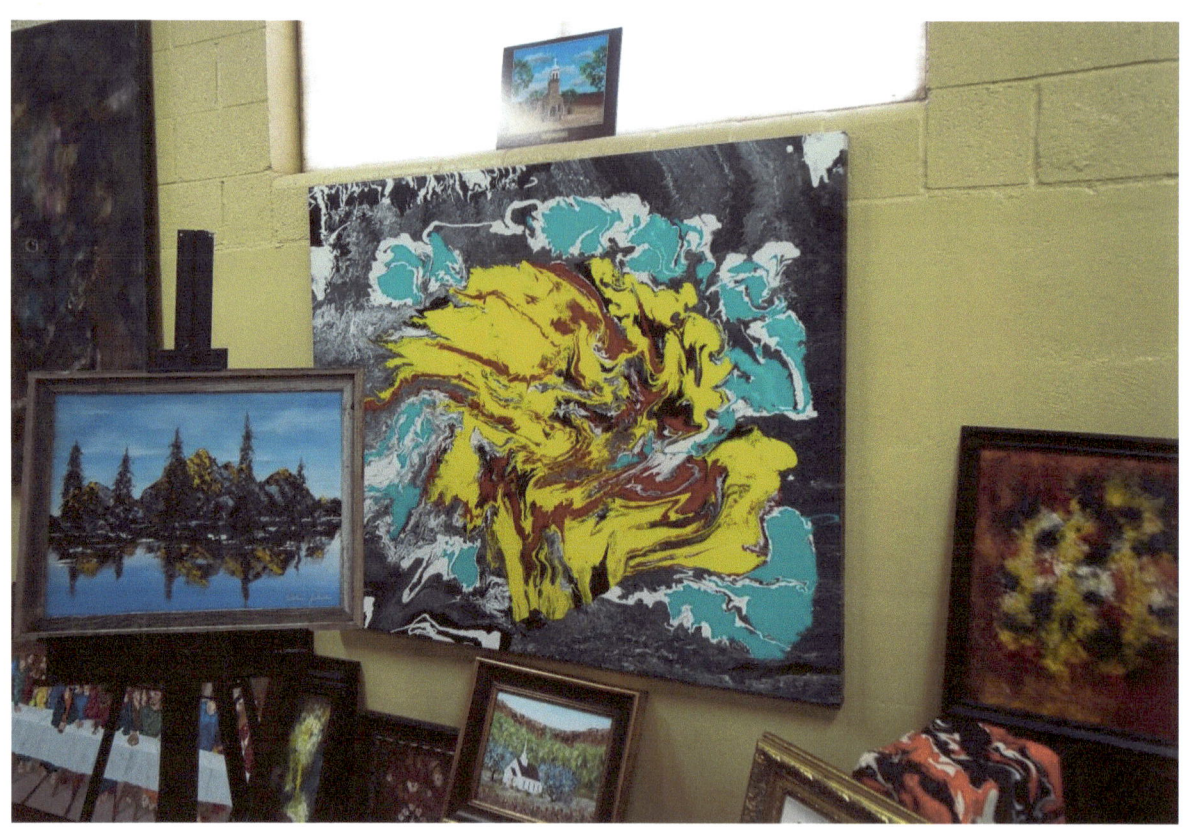

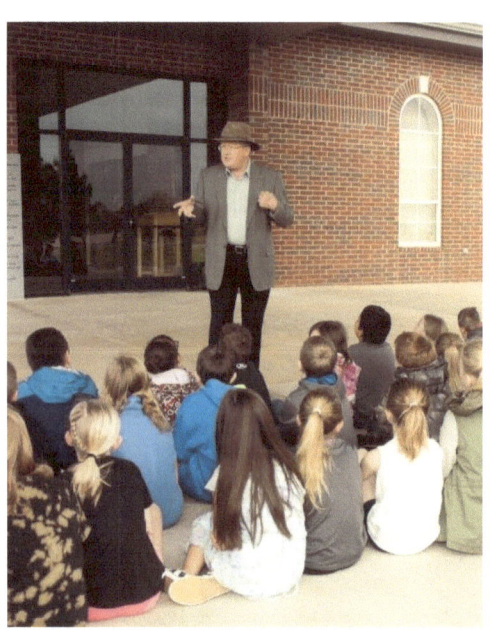

Is there an artist in you waiting to get out? The Van Gogh Gallery could be that still small voice that says, 'Call on me., I can do this."

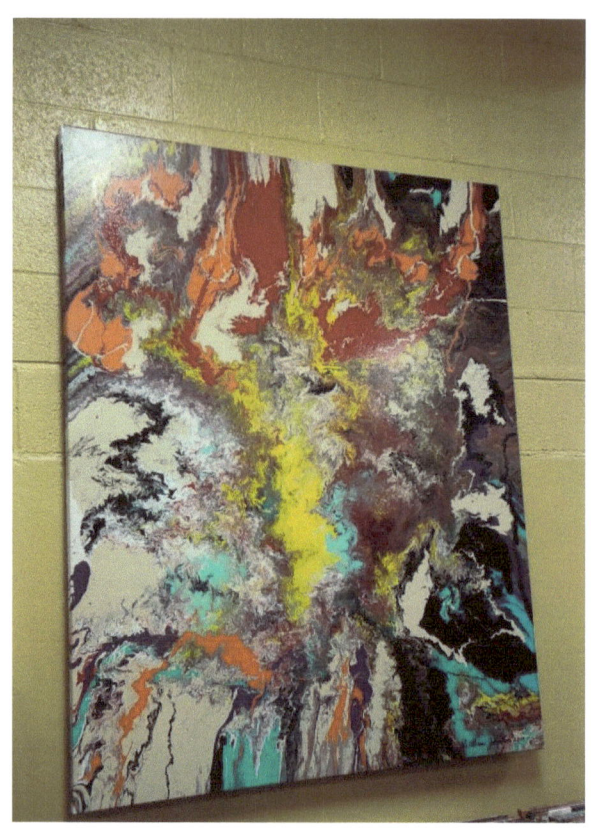

Schools, Churches, Social Clubs, Civic Clubs, Boys and Girls Groups, Youth Groups, Class Groups
Please call for appointment 580-478-3534. Visits to the Gallery are FREE - 7th and Walnut – Fairview, OK

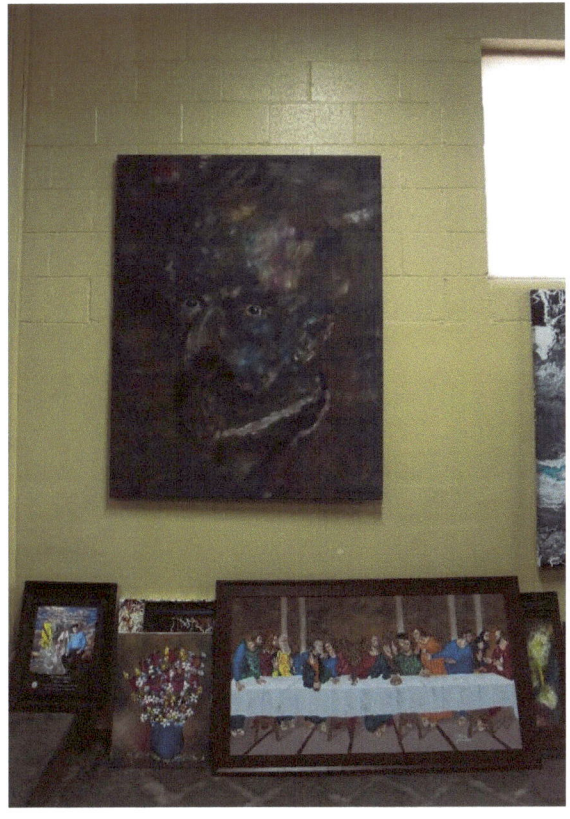

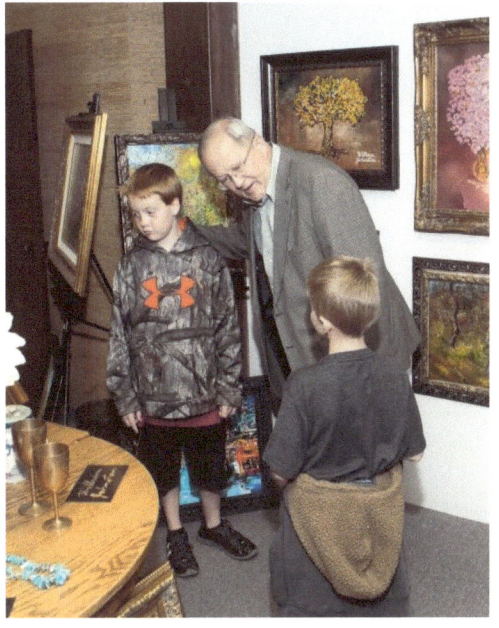

This is the world's most interesting gallery. Tours are FREE by appointment only. Call 580-478-3534

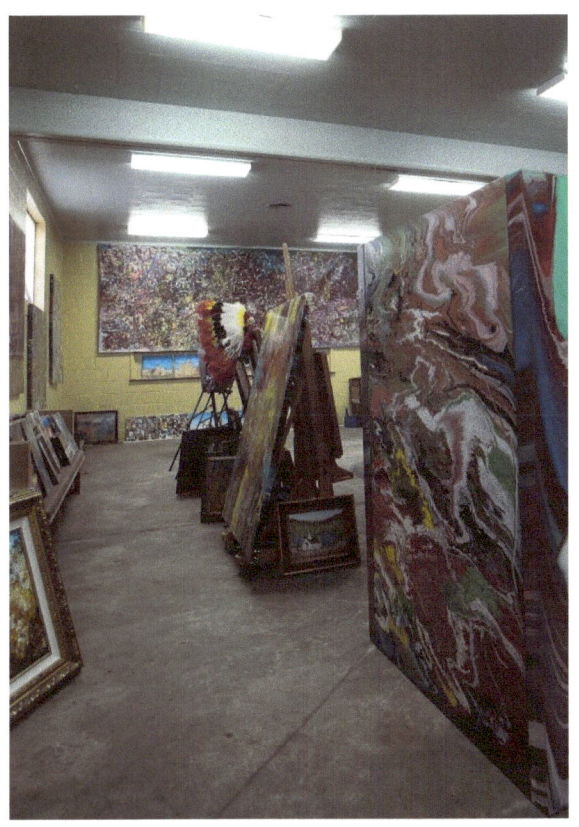

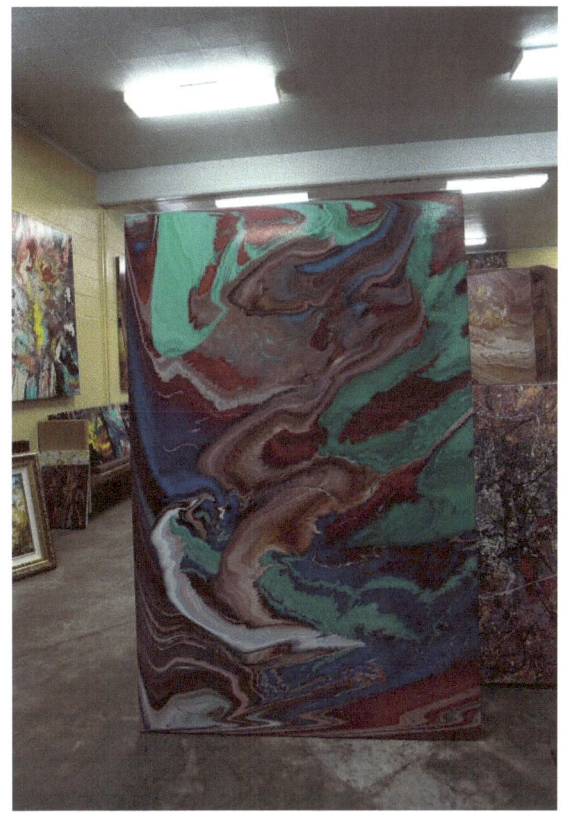

Schools, Churches, Social Clubs, Civic Clubs, Boys and Girls Groups, Youth Groups, Class Groups
Please call for appointment 580-478-3534. Visits to the Gallery are FREE - 7th and Walnut – Fairview, OK

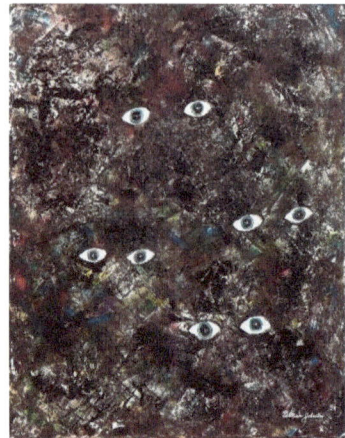
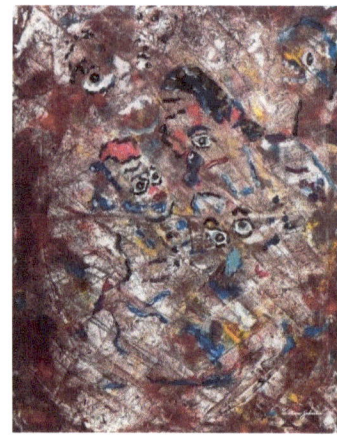
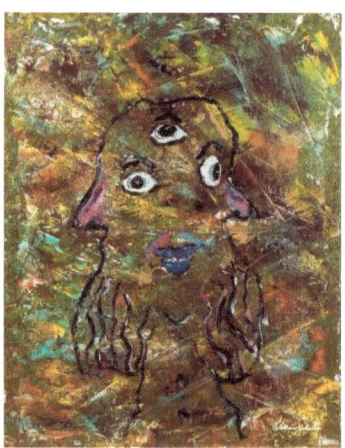

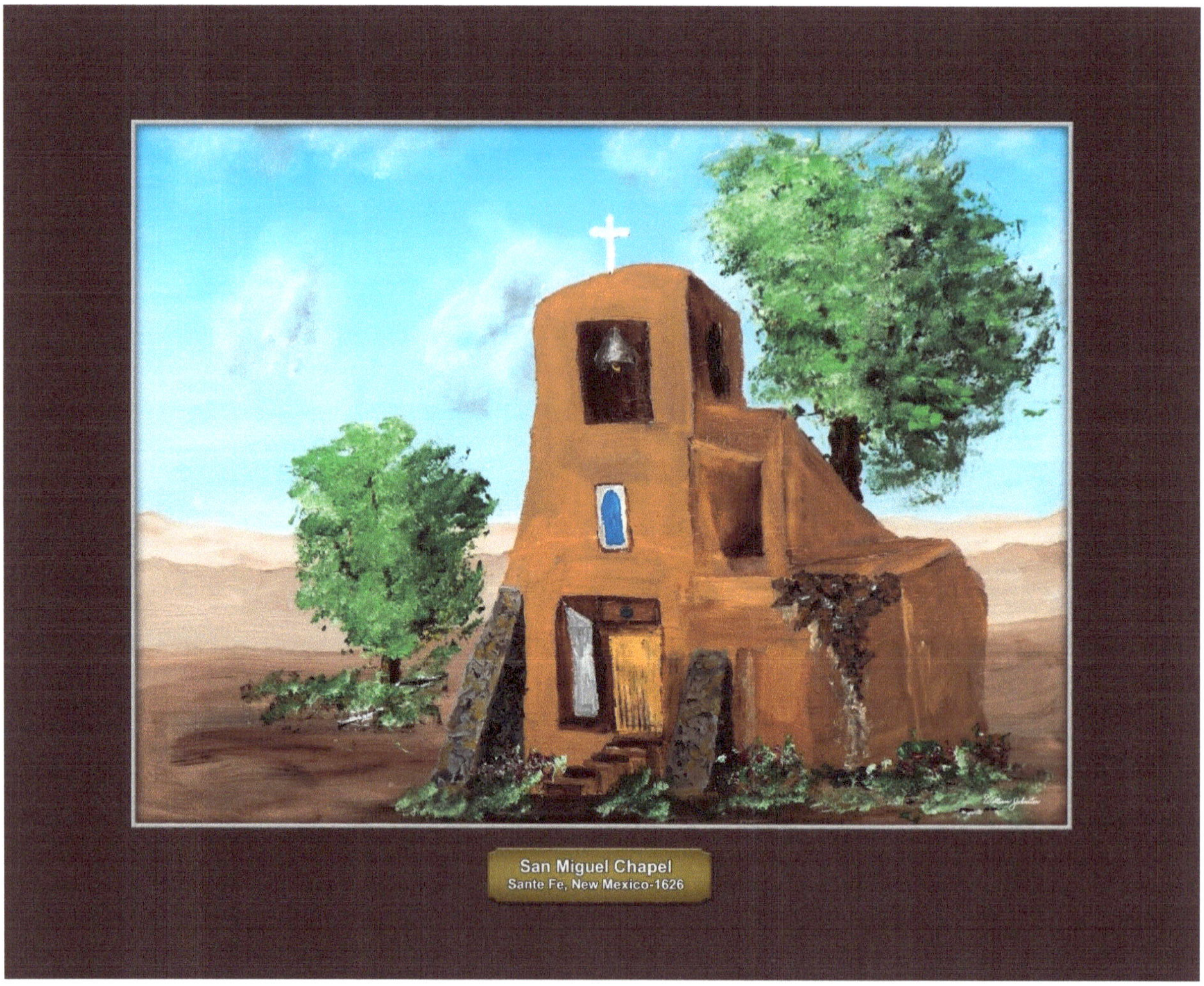

San Miguel Chapel
Sante Fe, New Mexico-1626

Schools, Churches, Social Clubs, Civic Clubs, Boys and Girls Groups, Youth Groups, Class Groups
Please call for appointment 580-478-3534. Visits to the Gallery are FREE - 7th and Walnut – Fairview, OK

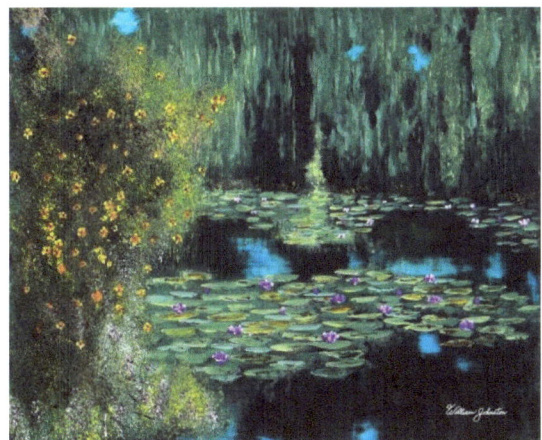
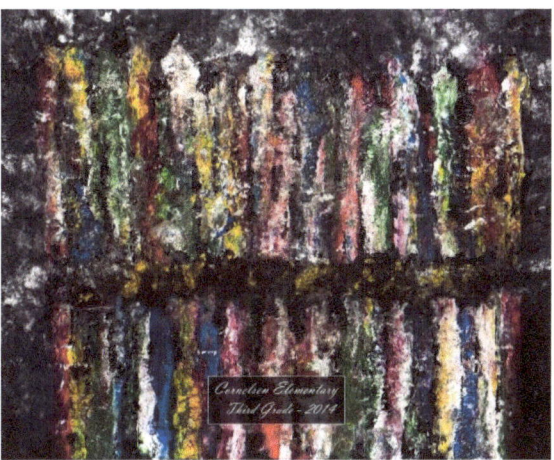

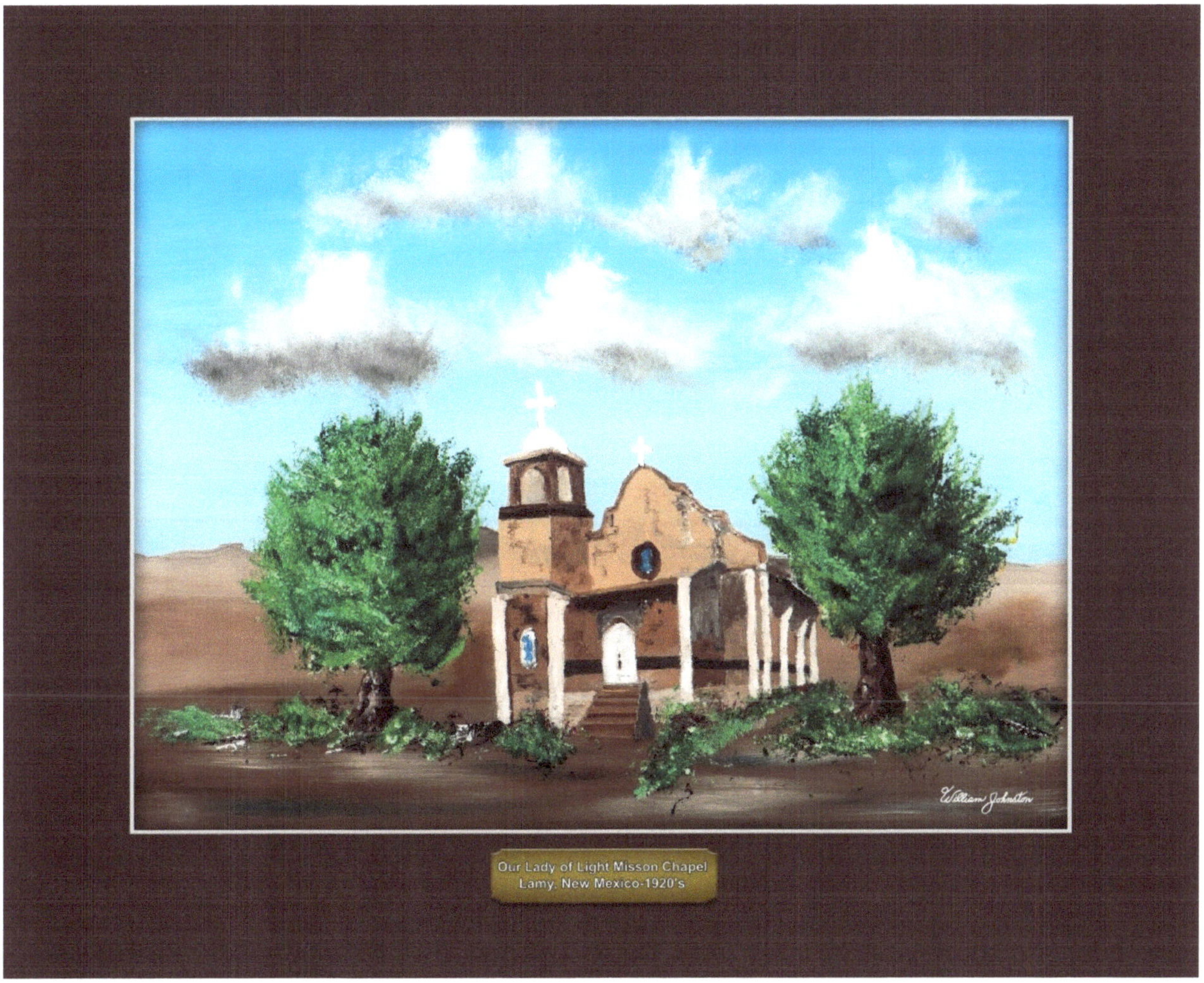

Our Lady of Light Mission Chapel
Lamy, New Mexico-1920's

Schools, Churches, Social Clubs, Civic Clubs, Boys and Girls Groups, Youth Groups, Class Groups
Please call for appointment 580-478-3534. Visits to the Gallery are FREE - 7th and Walnut – Fairview, OK

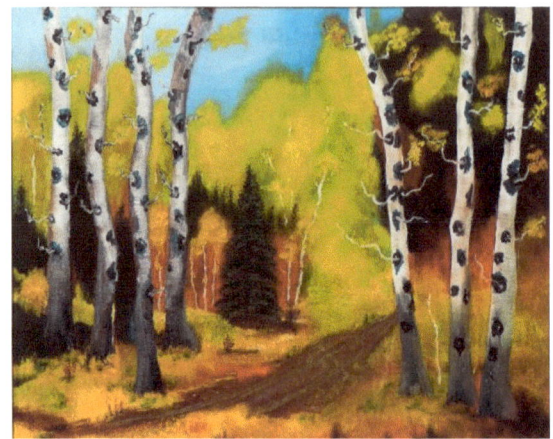
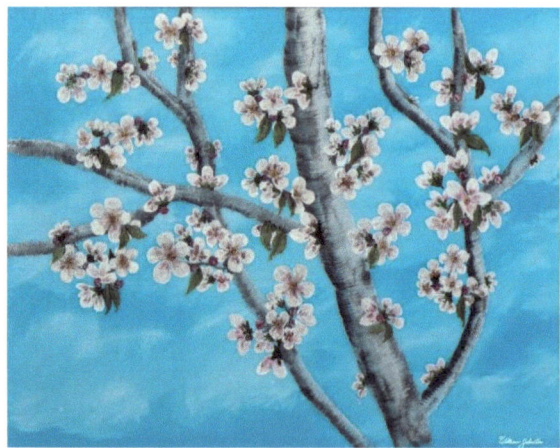

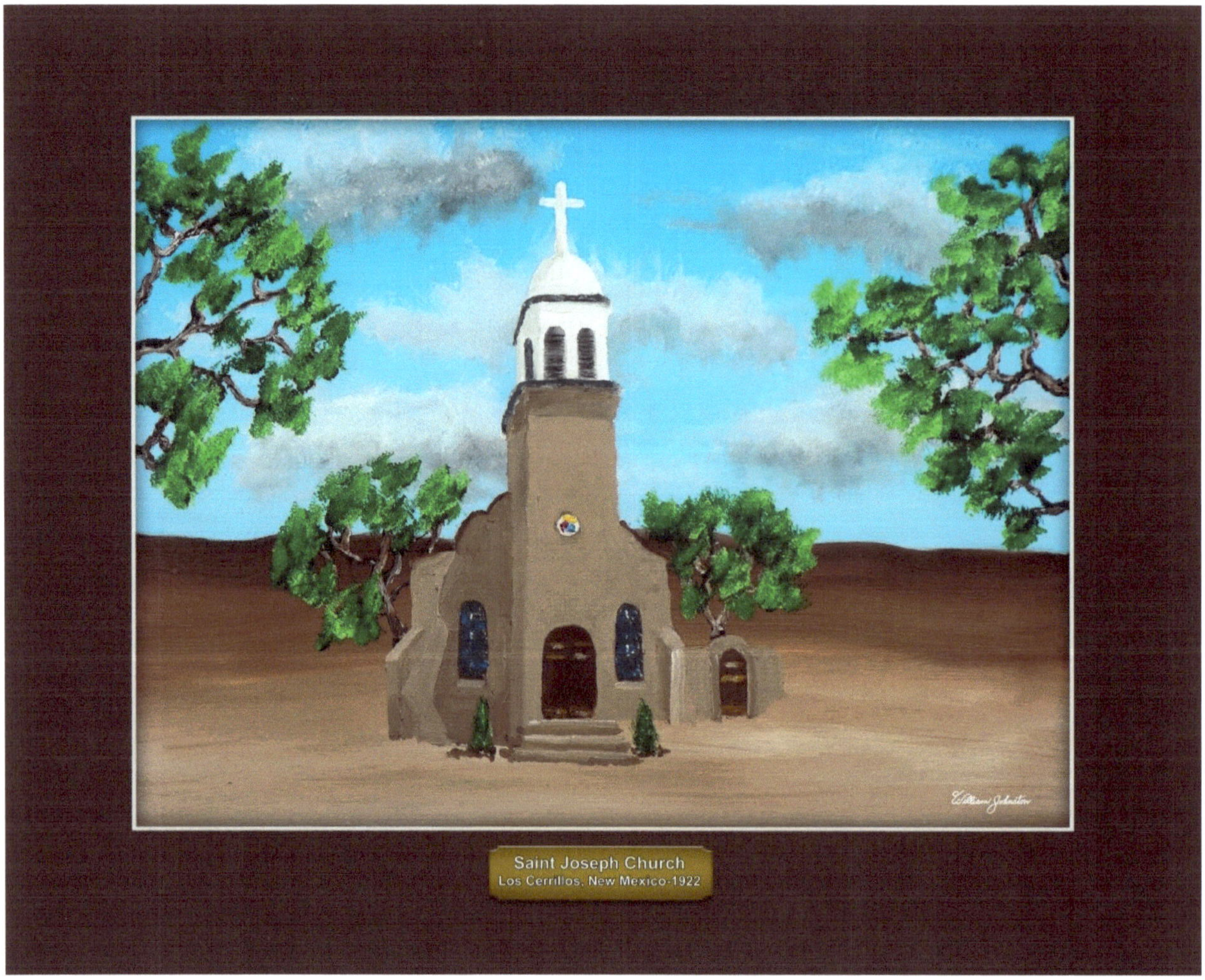

Saint Joseph Church
Los Cerrillos, New Mexico-1922

Schools, Churches, Social Clubs, Civic Clubs, Boys and Girls Groups, Youth Groups, Class Groups
Please call for appointment 580-478-3534. Visits to the Gallery are FREE - 7th and Walnut – Fairview, OK

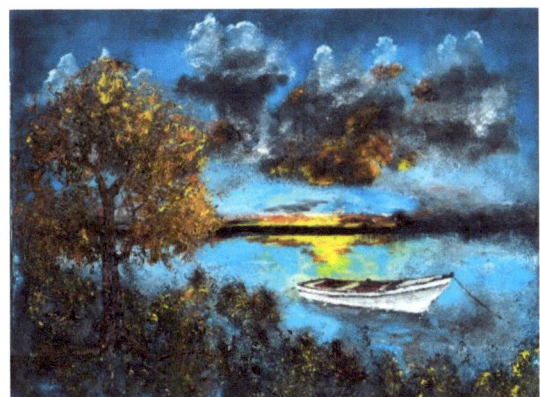
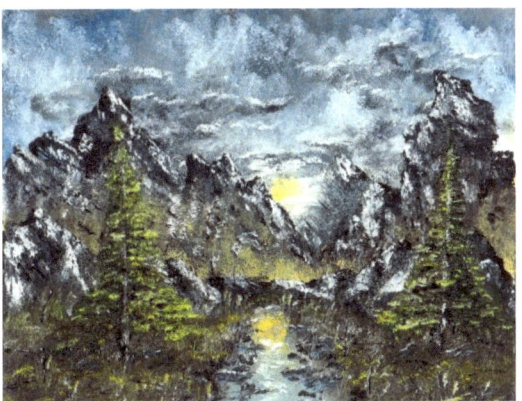

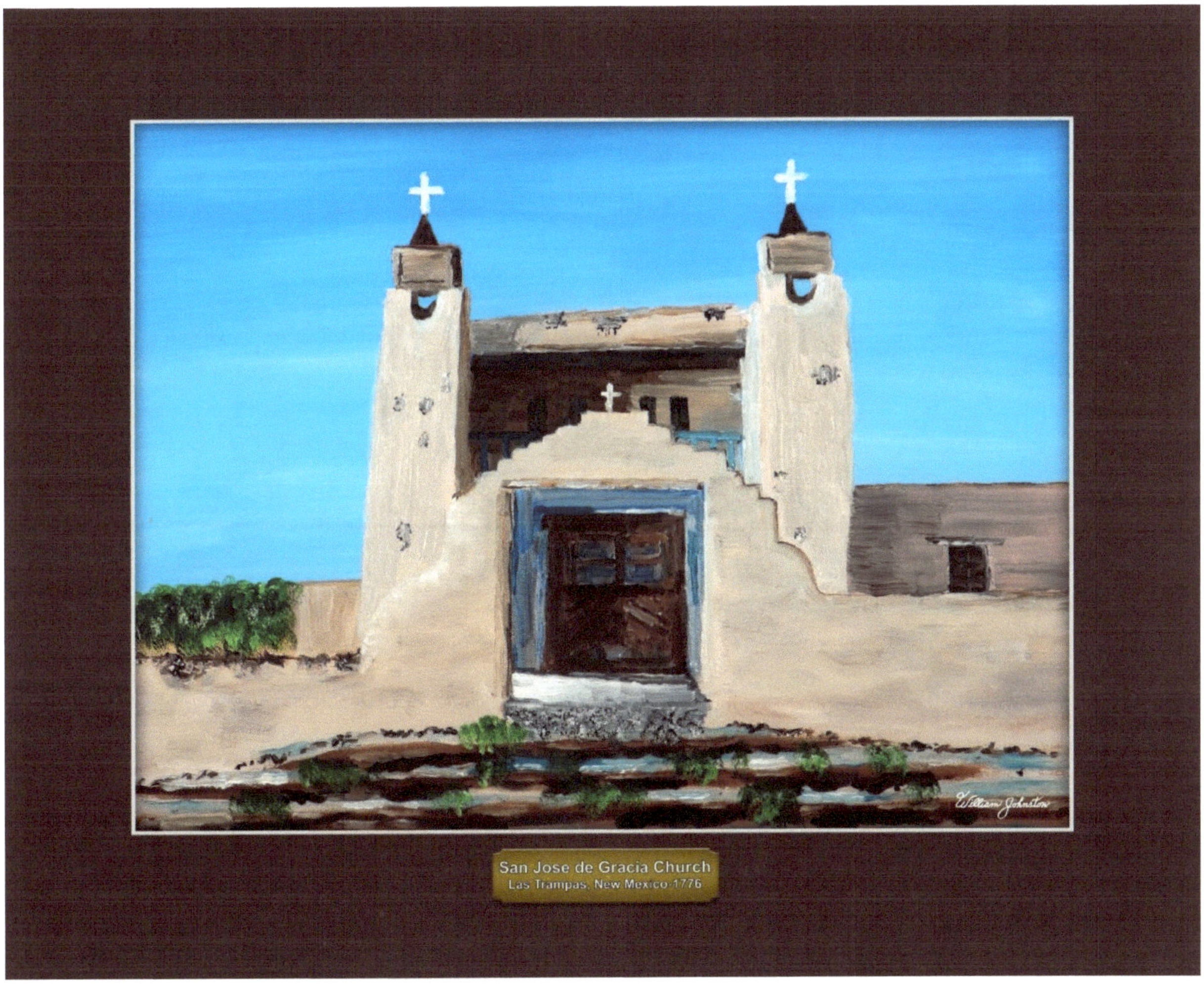

Schools, Churches, Social Clubs, Civic Clubs, Boys and Girls Groups, Youth Groups, Class Groups
Please call for appointment 580-478-3534. Visits to the Gallery are FREE - 7th and Walnut – Fairview, OK

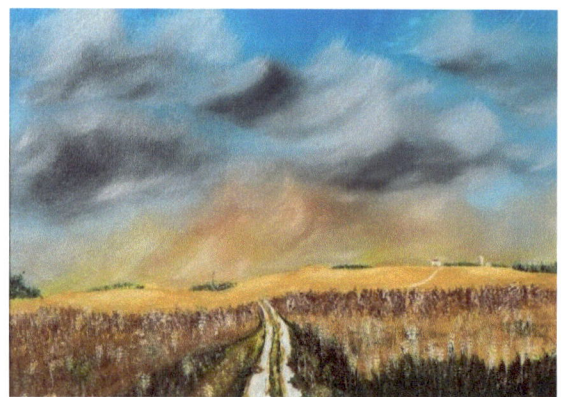
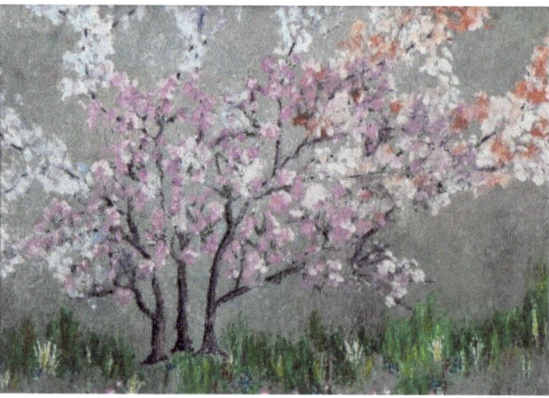

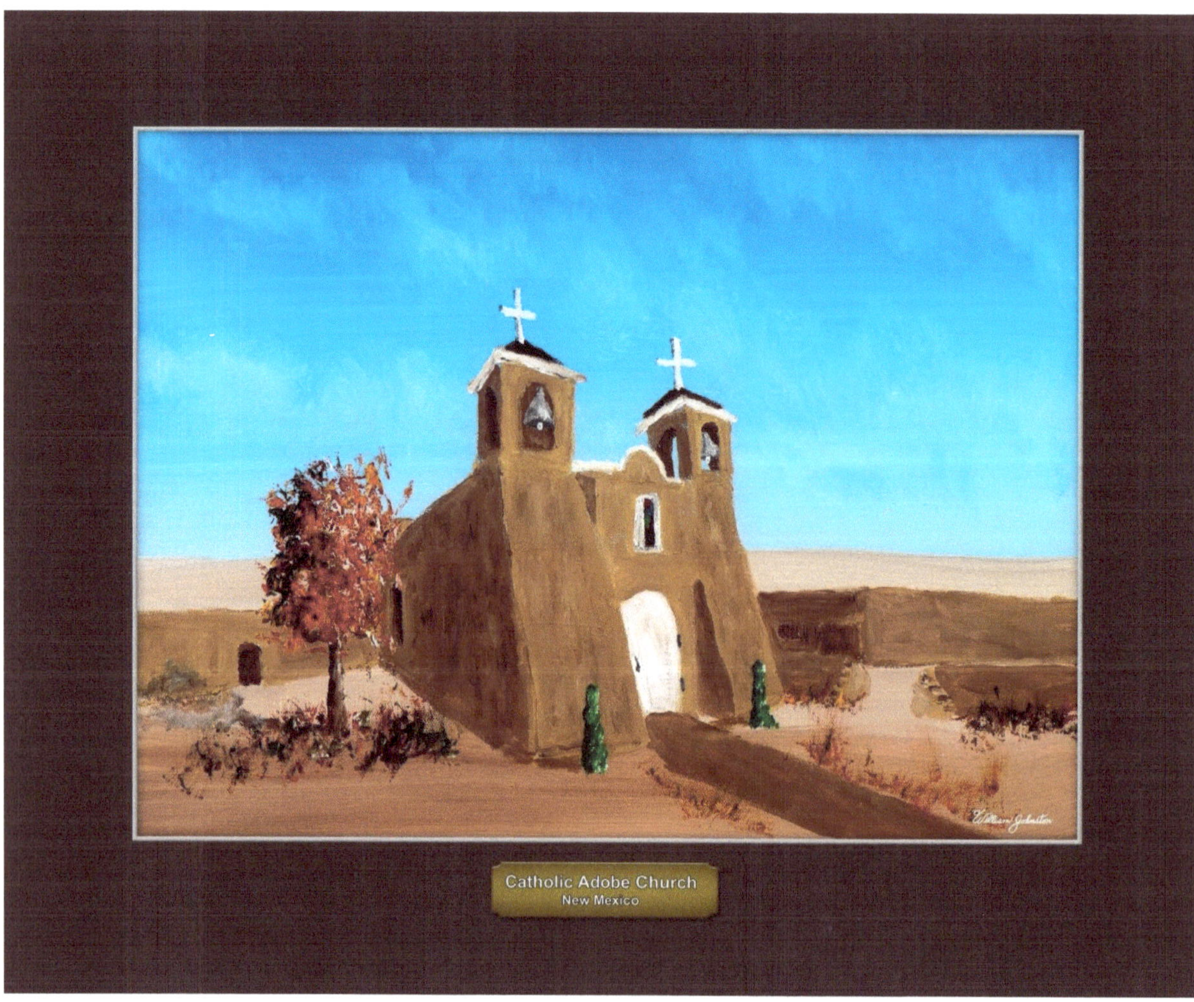

Catholic Adobe Church
New Mexico

Schools, Churches, Social Clubs, Civic Clubs, Boys and Girls Groups, Youth Groups, Class Groups
Please call for appointment 580-478-3534. Visits to the Gallery are FREE - 7th and Walnut – Fairview, OK

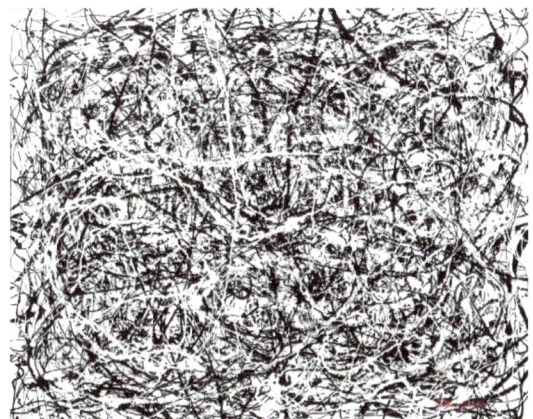
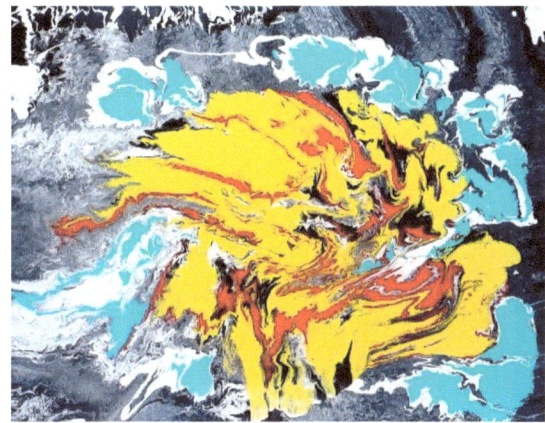

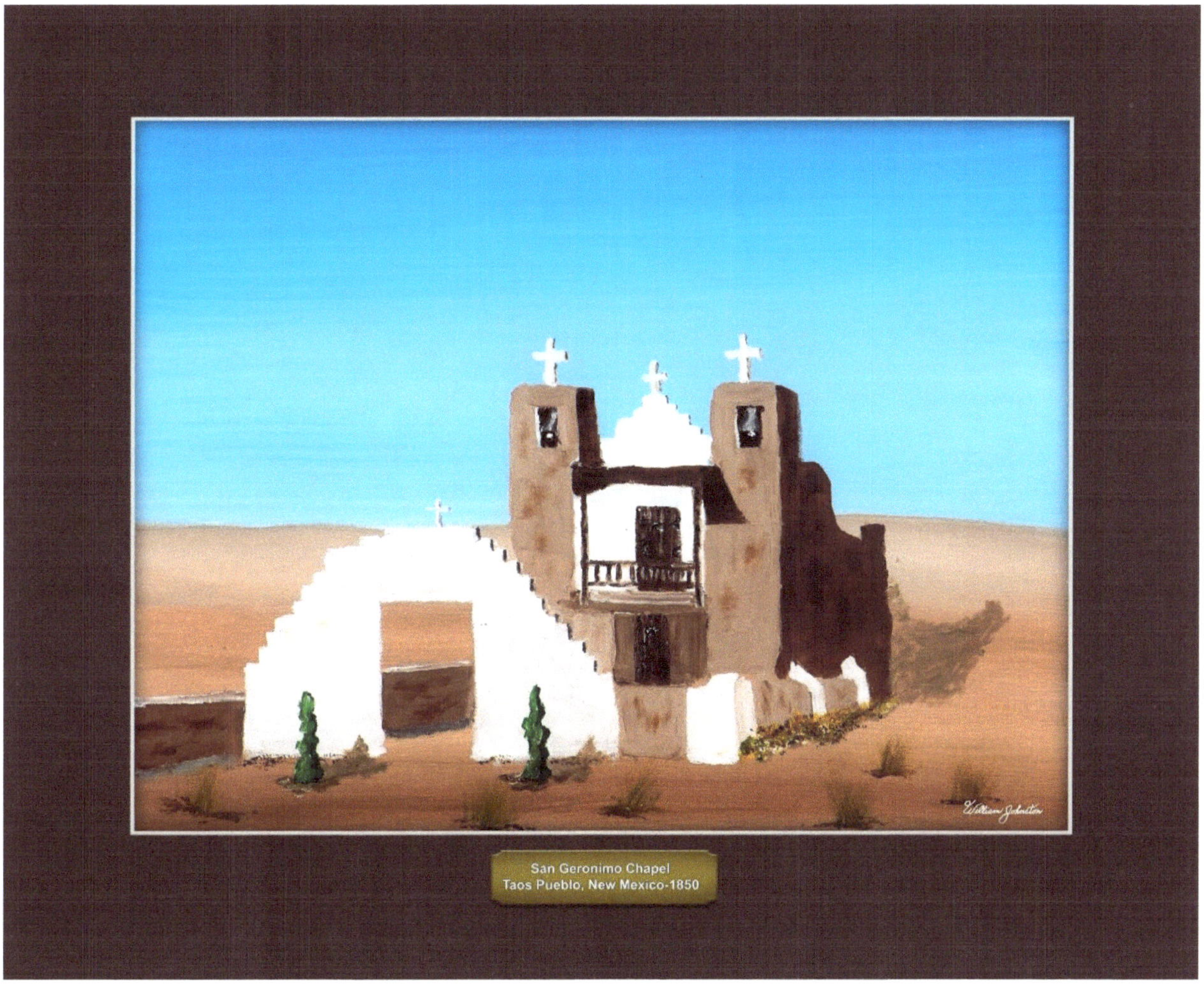

San Geronimo Chapel
Taos Pueblo, New Mexico-1850

Schools, Churches, Social Clubs, Civic Clubs, Boys and Girls Groups, Youth Groups, Class Groups
Please call for appointment 580-478-3534. Visits to the Gallery are FREE - 7th and Walnut – Fairview, OK

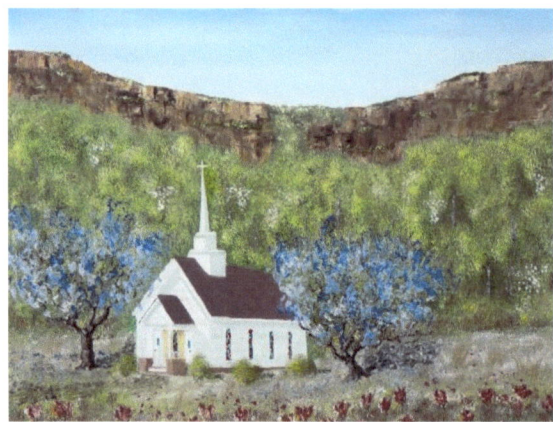
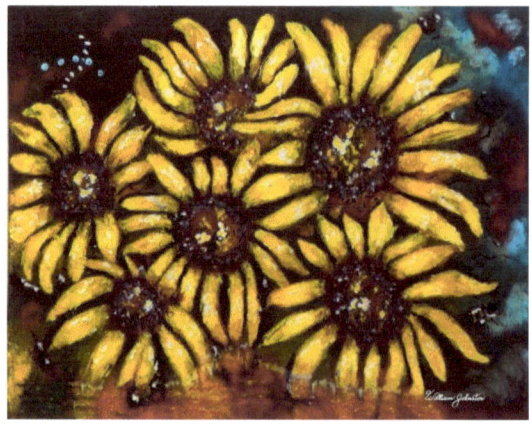

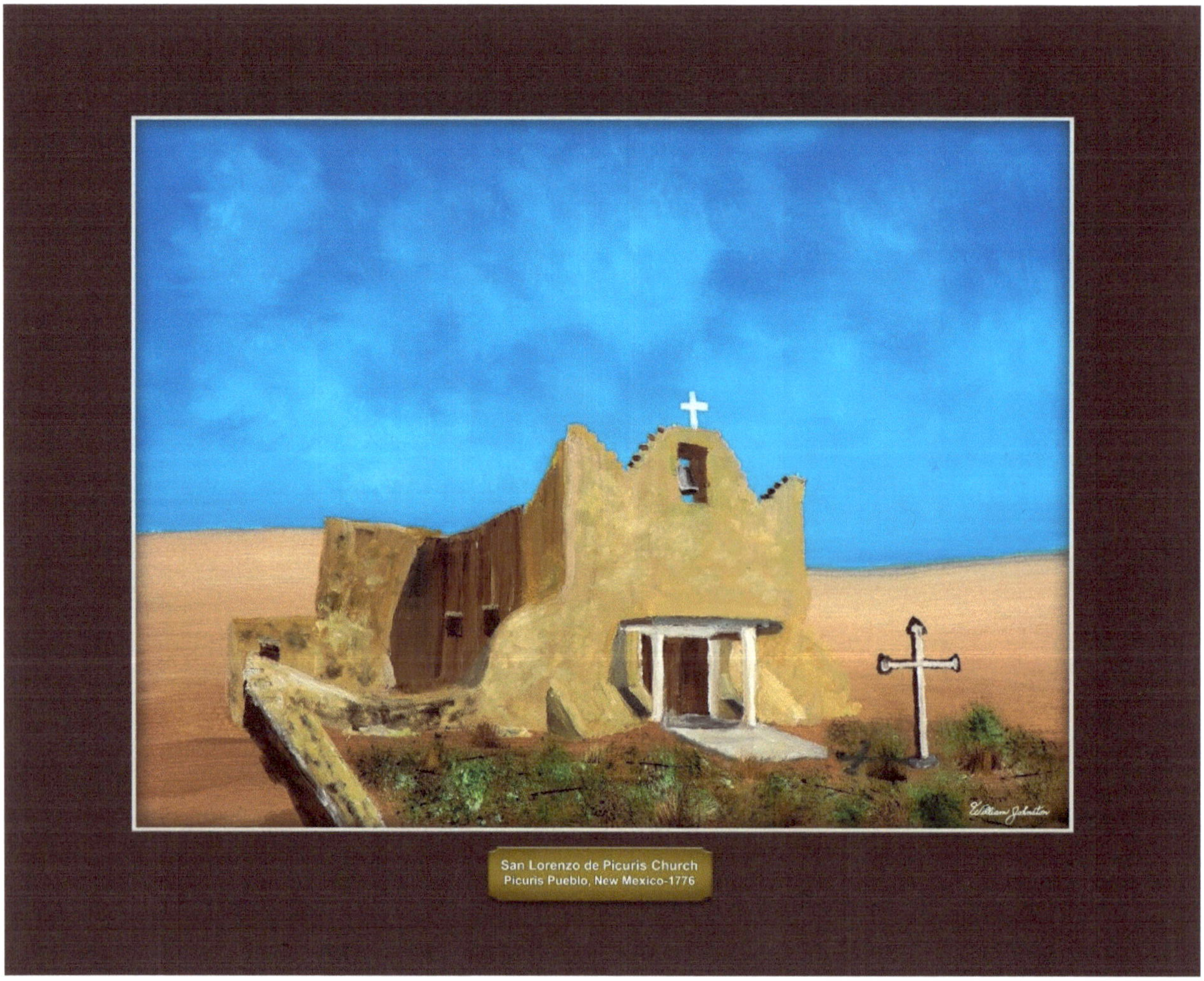

San Lorenzo de Picuris Church
Picuris Pueblo, New Mexico-1776

Schools, Churches, Social Clubs, Civic Clubs, Boys and Girls Groups, Youth Groups, Class Groups
Please call for appointment 580-478-3534. Visits to the Gallery are FREE - 7ᵗʰ and Walnut – Fairview, OK

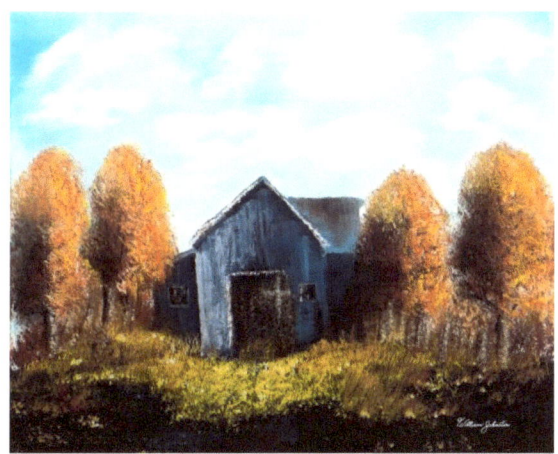
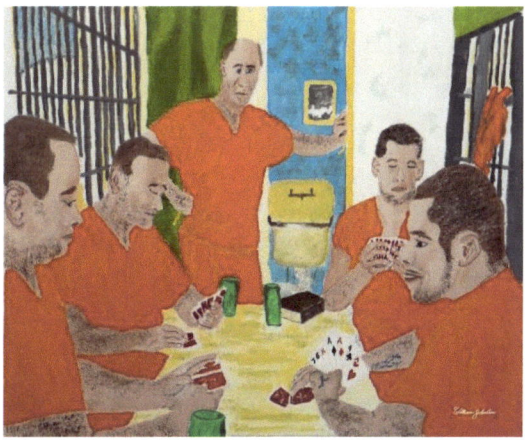
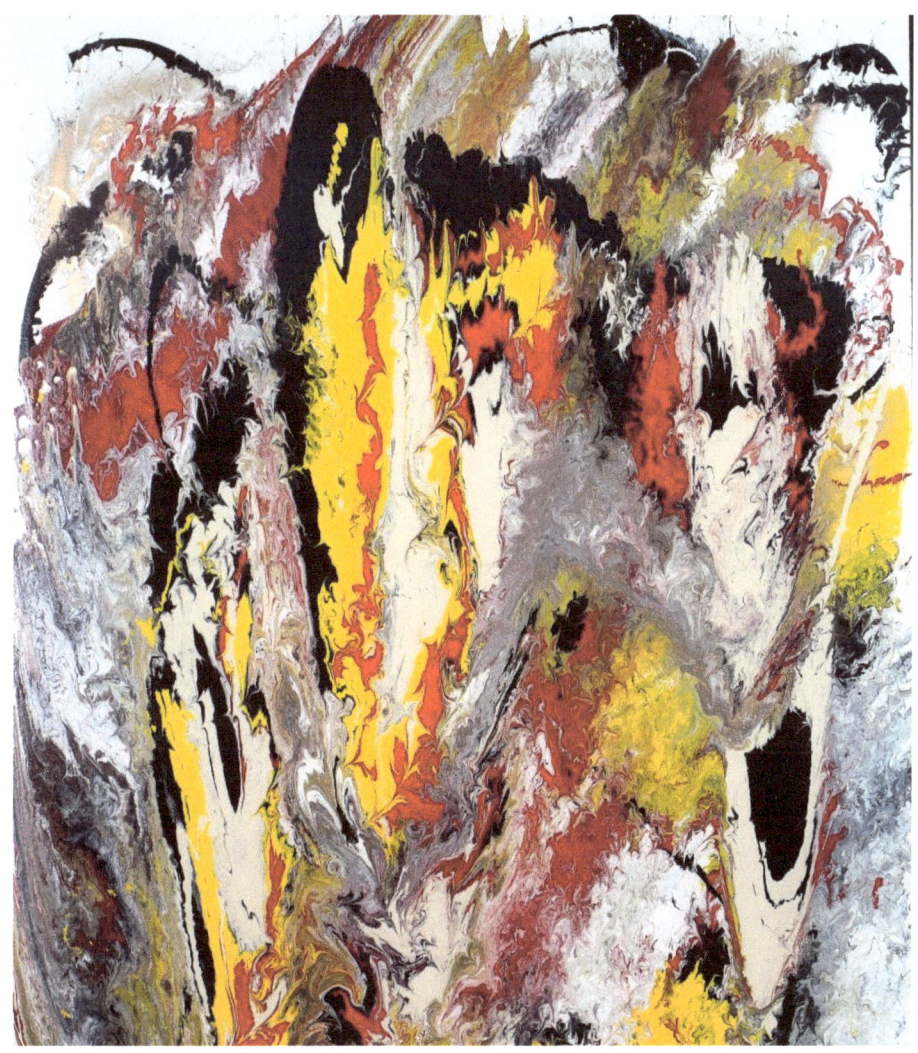

Schools, Churches, Social Clubs, Civic Clubs, Boys and Girls Groups, Youth Groups, Class Groups
Please call for appointment 580-478-3534. Visits to the Gallery are FREE - 7th and Walnut – Fairview, OK

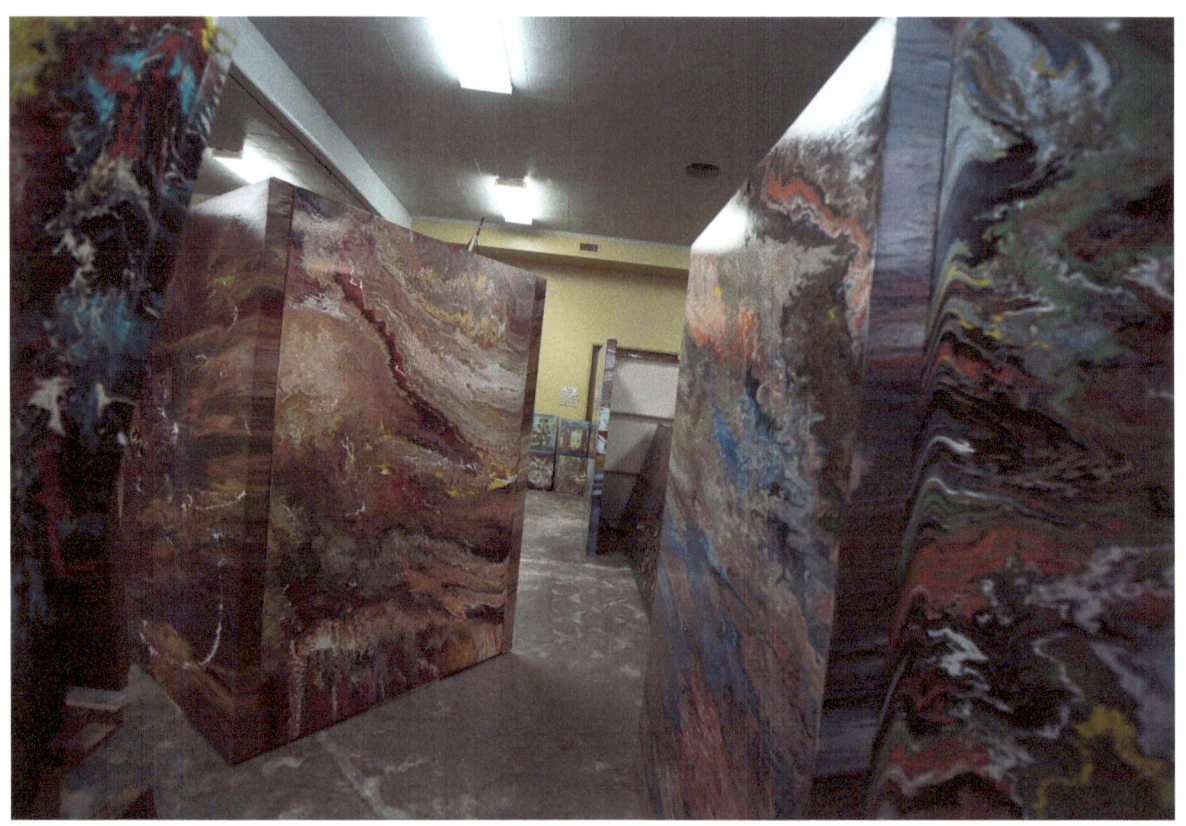

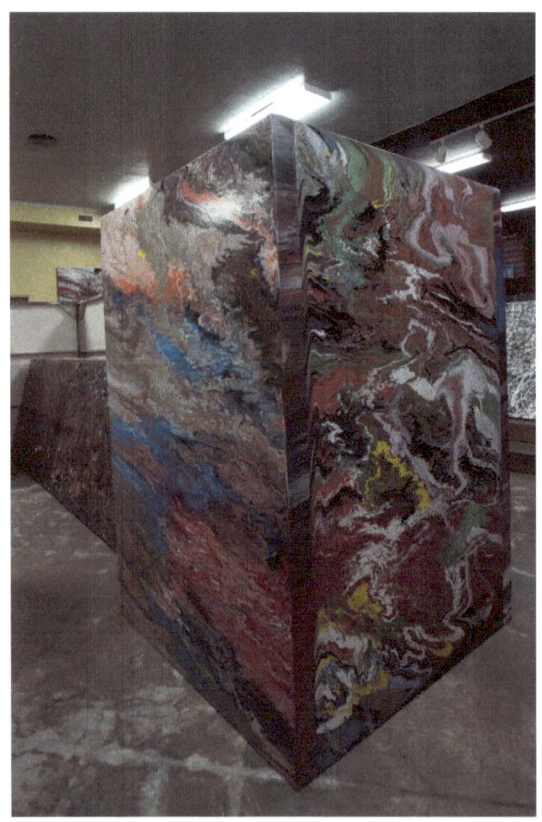

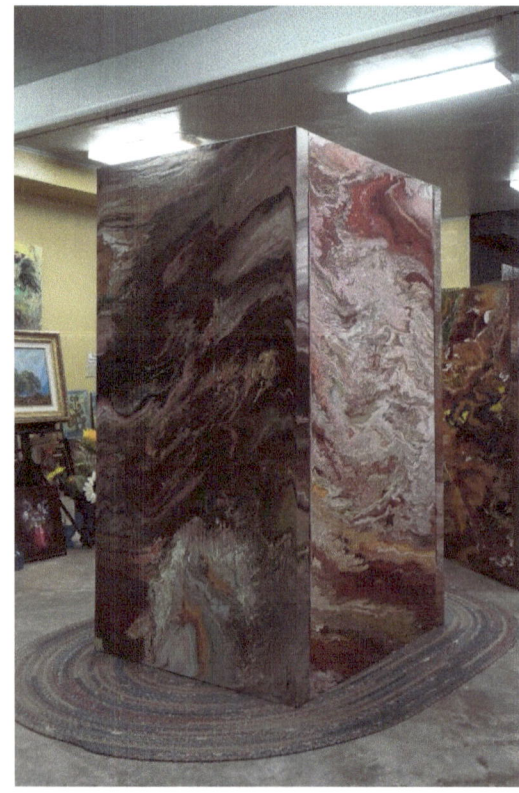